MONTESSORI

TODDLER

Learn To Parent The Right Way And
Help Your Kid Grow Independent,
Curious, And Educated With This
Montessori Positive Parenting Guide
With Strategies And Activities

NICOLA DAVIES

Follow me on my social
netwoks to receive
"Exclusive Bonuses"

MONTESSORI TODDLER DISCIPLINE

Copyright © 2022 by Nicola Davies.

ISBN: 9798357083722

This book is dedicated to Thomas and Danilo.
My most heartfelt love and source of inspiration.

We're here because of you

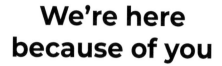

If you have found any value in this material, please consider leaving a review and joining the Author's Mission to give the most resourceful start to all children around the world

By scanning the QR-Code below ♥

★ ★ ★ ★ ★

SCAN ME

TABLE OF CONTENTS

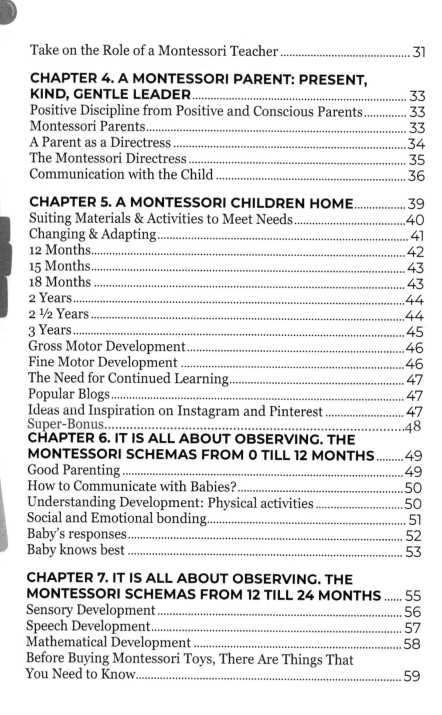

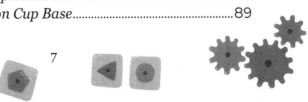

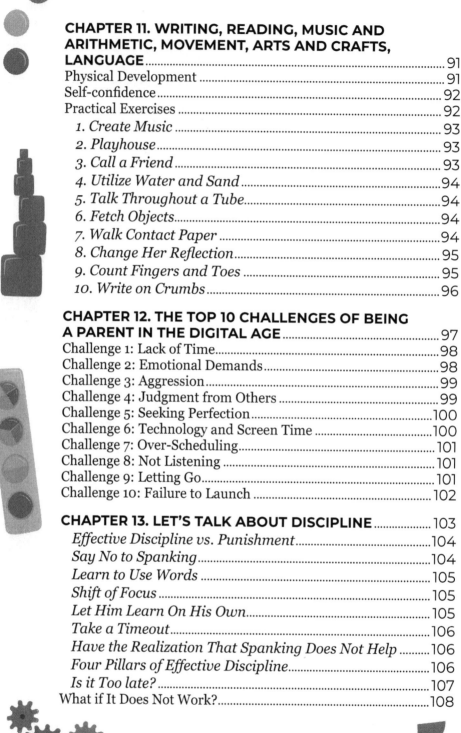

CHAPTER 11. WRITING, READING, MUSIC AND ARITHMETIC, MOVEMENT, ARTS AND CRAFTS, LANGUAGE

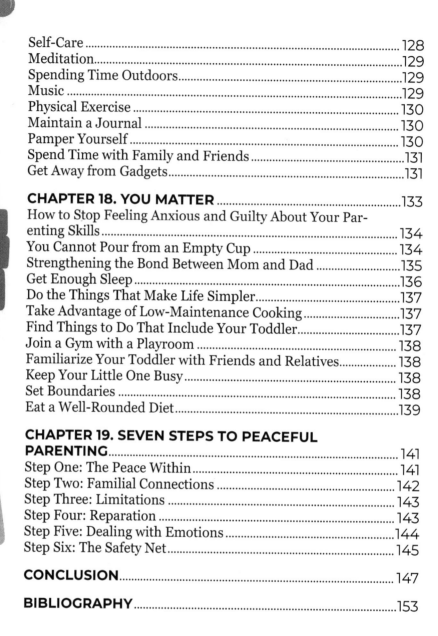

PREFACE

T his book is part of a series of manuscripts from the Mindful Parent Academy. This growing collection contains books that tackle various aspects of the life of modern parents with its inevitable challenges and unfathomable joys. All our books are driven by a compassionate, nonjudgmental, and positive approach that aim to support parents in their journey into parenthood, 'the most difficult job that comes without instructions but with plenty of expectations and demands'. At the heart of the Mindful Parent Academy there is a mission that is to shift the current trend that sees parents either feeling guilty and worried for spending too much time with their children to the detriment of their career. Or vice versa, a world where parents cannot spend enough time with their kids because of the strains put on them by their adult life and their job commitments. At the Mindful Parent Academy, we believe that any parent around the world should be put in favorable conditions in order to enjoy the right to be fully involved in this wonderful period of their child's life while being supported by the larger society. It is not a coincidence that in any given culture, in any part of the world, family (whoever this includes) is what drives people's actions and interests. Stressed by the demands of modern life and sleep deprived, often parents of the digital age risk to miss out on the absolute magic and delights of their child's early stages of life by leaving their toddlers to indulge in their favorite and hypnotizing digital content. However, the period such as toddlerhood, is increasingly recognized as the foundation for a happy, resilient, and confident adult life later. A delicate period where parents can really lay down the foundations for a healthy lifelong relationship with their children based on common values, rules, and respect for each other. Our mission

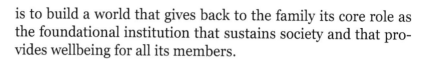

is to build a world that gives back to the family its core role as the foundational institution that sustains society and that provides wellbeing for all its members.

However, at the Mindful Parent Academy we believe that it is not just about the kid. We believe that there cannot be a flourishing tree without sturdy roots and that 'you cannot pour from an empty cup'. Therefore, whatever your circumstances, No Matter What, you must first look after your own well-being. And without guilt. We would like to introduce to your ways of keeping yourself mindful and positive with your children even when seriously sleep deprived, emotionally drained and juggling between the many demands of life. Keep yourself sane by finding time to look after yourself whatever that means in a given day: listening to your favorite podcasts on headphones while doing the dishes, repeating positive mantras while changing dirty nappies, doing on-line (and possibly live) exercises classes for mums (dads can join too), reflect and write down the rules and values that you most care about and discuss them with other relevant carers so to agree, updating your gratitude list, read a paragraph (or even a line) of your favorite book before falling asleep, give yourself permission to cry and let it go, going to the woods or for a walk on your own even when it's starting to rain, singing nursery rhymes with your kids at the top of your voice and join in with the actions, connect yourself and your kids to nature even by just watering the plants or repotting them to bigger pots, dancing with your kids like no one is watching, and much, much more.. At the Mindful Parent Academy, we have your well-being at heart. You must try every possible way to keep yourself calm, happy, connected, and sane while the demands put on you as a carer and provider are never ending and your energy and patience are fluctuating. Enjoy your reading.

INTRODUCTION

This book combines the Montessori Method for children with the mindful and positive discipline approach for parents. The Montessori Method was developed over 100 years ago by Maria Montessori, the Italian physician and educator. Montessori has developed a practical framework for the application of her theory. Her creativity in this regard is a significant explanation for the long-lasting and pervasive influence of her work. It should be borne in mind, though, that Montessori intended her approach to be considered an open-minded, not a predetermined program. She believed in creativity in the classroom, and her entire approach to teaching was in the spirit of continuous exploration focused on the child's insight.

Furthermore, this book also suggests that a comprehensive cognitive development goes hand in hand with a healthy emotional development and suggests adopting a mindful approach in order to foster a positive parenting discipline. The book will explain the importance of being mindful as a precondition for a positive parenting approach. What does it actually mean to be (or aspire to be) a Positive and Mindful parent in the current world and how it can be linked to a guilt-free approach?

The book will point at ways to try and reach a No Drama No Yelling home by establishing clear and solid boundaries while creating an emotional connection and warmth within them. The book will explore ways to communicate and connect with your toddler/s, the tools to redirect their actions, the tricks to recognize the triggers of a tantrum and avoid them, but also how to teach your children how to be responsible, respectful and cooperative. The main aim of this work is to equip all parents with the tools to manage their parenthood journey, knowing what

to expect so that they can handle most situations in a calm and constructive way, avoiding yelling, establishing respect, managing tantrums while remaining deeply connected with their children and build that 'wonder-full' lifelong relationship that you will be so proud of. Let's begin!

CHAPTER 1

WHAT WE NEED TO KNOW ABOUT TODDLERS' AND THEIR BRAIN DEVELOPMENT?

I t is pretty amazing when you realize that right when your child is born into the world that they become aware of their surroundings, even though they may not be able to determine what is precisely happening properly. The precious beauty of the toddler stage is you get to watch first-hand as your child learns to explore the world that is around them. These are the ages in which they truly begin to build an understanding of people and objects, as well as learning with their bodies, home, and world functions.

While there are interesting changes physically within your toddler that you can see on the outside, there are even more drastic developments occurring within their rapidly expanding brains as they learn how to take in and interpret the world around them. As they are making strides in observing and successfully interacting with objects and people, their brains become more and more capable of processing, storing, and utilizing vital information.

Toddler and Their Brain Development

Ages 1–2 Years

- ✓ They can feel proud and accomplished when they have completed something independently.
- ✓ They understand the difference between "me" and "you."
- ✓ They can recognize objects that are familiar to them.
- ✓ They are capable of matching similar objects.
- ✓ They enjoy short and simple story time.

- Storytime for kids means getting to snuggle up next to Mom and/or Dad, look at cool pictures, and hear interesting sounds as parents read. Your kids are learning the following:
- Stories have both a beginning and an end.
- Books can tell stories.
- Reading properly involves doing so from left to right.
- How the books work from the beginning then to how the story works.

- ✓ They can understand and respond to words and commands.
- ✓ They start to imitate the words and actions of adults.
- ✓ They highly enjoy dancing to music.
- ✓ They recognize what the term "no" means and begins to use it properly.
- ✓ They can recognize who they are in the mirror or other reflections.

Ages 2–3 Years

- ✓ They have learned to count "1-2-3."
- ✓ They have the capability to inform others of their actions.
- ✓ They can identify themselves in the mirror with their name.
- ✓ They can put together simple 3- to 4-piece puzzles.
- ✓ They are more than capable of stacking rings on peg toys in order of size.
- ✓ They play pretend with dolls, stuffed animals, or other toys.
- ✓ They can group objects by categories (food, clothing, and animals).

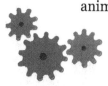

✓ They can name off objects in books or magazines.
✓ They respond effectively to simple directions.
✓ They understand simple stories.

Cognitive Red Flags to Be Aware

If you take note of some of the following things by the time your child reaches the ages of 18–24 months, you may want to speak with your doctor.

Ages 1–2 Years

✓ They require the need for constant, undivided attention to stay at an activity.
✓ They constantly go from one activity to another and is unable to stay absorbed in an activity for very long.
✓ They are interested in feeling or watching toys rather than playing, interacting, or using them.
✓ They never imitate other individuals.
✓ They do not grasp the function of common objects ("find something to eat" instead of "find a cookie").
✓ They begin to understand empathy.

• Toddlers are beginning to make connections between not only their feelings but also the feelings of others. This is crucial in building relationships and friendships now and in the future.
• Do not put an emotional band-aid over them when they feel bad or sad about something they did or something that has occurred. Your child must learn how to cope by adequately identifying with their emotions. Reassure them that it is okay that they feel the way they do.

Ages 2–3 Years

✓ They need undivided attention to stay within an activity.
✓ They move from one activity to another.
✓ They continue using mouth toys and have no interest in playing with toys.

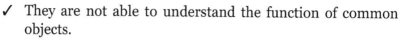

- ✓ They are not able to understand the function of common objects.
- ✓ They are unable to practice basic categorization successfully.
- ✓ They have no interest in wanting to participate in pretend play.

Strides in Independence

By the time your little one has spawned into walking and slightly talking human beings, they are already making strides in gaining their independence. With the realization that they can do quite a few simple tasks on their very own, they tend to venture to do their things. It is crucial to give your child plenty of room and opportunities to grow.

- ✓ When it is necessary, be firm with your toddler. When you need them to abide by your rules and in your way, ensure that you are communicating this to them quickly and deliberately, yet calmly as well. For example, once your child is properly restrained in the means of their car seat, you can inform them of the reasons why they are buckled into one, include the dangers but do not frighten them with gory details.
- ✓ Tell your little one "yes" whenever you possibly can, if you are sure, they are not in any grave danger or injuring or drastically harming themselves.
- ✓ Patience is key and curbing the need to assist your child will come with practice. But let them use their eating utensils and let them pull down their pants. They will learn!
- ✓ Ensure that you include them when it comes to chore time. Show and let them hold the dustpan. Give them a rag or duster to get down and dust things at their level.
- ✓ Make plenty of room in your hectic schedule for your toddler to do certain things at a pace that is comfortable for them. If they want to dress by themselves, let them. If they want to attempt to put on their shoes, by all means! Just remember that leaving your house will inevitably take longer until they get the hang of these tasks.

From Birth to 3 Years of Age

The roots of the youngsters' development are set during the initial three years of their life. Montessori considers this period one of a "profound embryo," in which the youngster observes, does, and experiments. This procedure is accomplished by the youngster's "retentive psyche," which joins relations, feelings, pictures, language, and culture through their faculties and by the straightforward reality of living. These educational encounters shape their mind, their framing systems of neurons that have the capability of remaining with the individual for all their life. From birth to 3 years of age, the Montessori training is also focused on the improvement of talking that facilitate development and autonomy, gives the kid confidence, and permits them to find their underlying capacities and their place inside a network.

20

CHAPTER 2

THE FIVE MONTESSORI PRINCIPLES

Rule 1: Respect for the Child

Regard for the Child is the most significant rule hidden behind the whole Montessori Method (not basic practice in the mid-twentieth century). Regard is express by not interfering with their fixation. Additionally, regard is express by allowing students to settle on decisions, to get things done for themselves, and to also learn for themselves. The most important instruction for the Montessori adult is to respect all pulpils and learn to observe without judgment.

Rule 2: The Absorbent Mind

Montessori training is based on the rule that, essentially, by living, kids are continually gaining from their general surroundings. Through their faculties, youngsters continually assimilate data from their reality. They understand it since they are thinking creatures.

Rule 3: Sensitive Periods

The Montessori teaching method considers certain periods when youngsters are progressively prepared to gain proficiency with specific abilities. These are delicate periods when is essential for the youngster to persevere to gain the skills. These deli-

cate periods change for every youngster. Through their perception, Montessori educators must distinguish delicate periods in their pulpils and give the right assets to kids to thrive during this time.

Rule 4: The Prepared Environment

The Montessori Method proposes that youngsters learn best in a situation that has been set up to empower them to get things done for themselves. Continuously kid-focused, the learning condition ought to elevate opportunity for youngsters to freely investigate materials. Instructors ought to set up the learning condition by making materials accessible to kids deliberately and autonomously.

Rule 5: Auto training

Auto instruction, or self-training, is the idea that kids are fit for teaching themselves. This is one of the most significant convictions in the Montessori Method. Montessori instructors give the motivation, the direction, and the support for youngsters to teach themselves.

Arranged Environment

The Montessori approach gives an appealing and deliberately arranged condition to exploit the pinnacle time of affectability toward learning. It is particularly intended to address the kid's questions and animate his interest. Quality, simplicity, attempt, and sensible request are fundamental traits of homeroom materials if kids are to be attracted to investigate and gain from them.

The Prepared Environment is equipped with a studied arrangement of self-showing instructive materials that fulfil the youngster's ability while shielding the person in question from pointless disappointment. The kid is allowed to participate in "unconstrained action" with most extreme freedom from the grown-ups and with the advantage of friends who can likewise help in the learning.

Numerous Montessori exercises, particularly at toddler level with the most solid students, are intended to cause the child to notice the tactile properties of items: size, shape, shading, surface, weight, smell, sound, and so forth. Step by step, toddlers figure out how to focus cautiously, seeing even more unmistakably little subtleties in the things around them. They have started to watch and value their condition. This is key in helping the kid find hows and to learn.

Self-rule

Opportunity is a pre-imperative condition for learning. A free youngster is one who is building up their latent capacity and wants to work out issues; yet he is fit for requesting and accepting heading when important. Opportunity does not suggest that youngster may fiercely do whatever, at whatever point the person in question needs; it alludes to the demonstration of duty and sensibly picking one's game-plan, among many offered, whitin a characterized set of limits.

The Montessori Method accepts that every youngster is completely fit for instructing oneself and appreciates learning through development and experience of opportunity when their rights are regarded. The desire of the grown-ups is not forced on them.

If they knew the words, even small kids would state, "assist me with figuring out how to do it without your help!"

Order

Order is the second pre-imperative condition for learning; it is the inward, individual drive to make and keep up an inside feeling of direction and inspiration. Control alludes to the capacity to direct one's conduct intentionally and worthily by utilizing the Prepared Environment.

Montessori depends on significant regard for a kid's character, where the individual in question works from the free decision and is permitted a portion of autonomy—this structure the premise of internal order. The youngster builds up their posi-

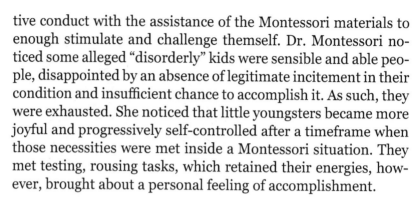

tive conduct with the assistance of the Montessori materials to enough stimulate and challenge themself. Dr. Montessori noticed some alleged "disorderly" kids were sensible and able people, disappointed by an absence of legitimate incitement in their condition and insufficient chance to accomplish it. As such, they were exhausted. She noticed that little youngsters became more joyful and progressively self-controlled after a timeframe when those necessities were met inside a Montessori situation. They met testing, rousing tasks, which retained their energies, however, brought about a personal feeling of accomplishment.

Basic Thinking

Montessori centers on instructing and learning for comprehension, and bravely holding onto fails as normal strides in the learning procedure. The Montessori Method instructs kids to fundamentally think, not just to retain, criticize, and overlook. As opposed to giving replacements heaps of right answers, Montessori instruction continues posing the correct inquiries to lead the learner to find the responses for themselves from the materials. Learning turns into its prize, and every achievement power a craving to find significantly more.

Kids will figure out how to reinforce their social and enthusiastic turn of events. Kids figure out how to bargain and be aware. Preschool gives a domain to youngsters to investigate, increase a feeling of self, play with friends, and assemble fearlessness. Kids learn they can achieve assignments and settle on choices without the assistance of their folks.

Brain development is continuous and begins even before the child is born. So, children need to improve their mental skills and talent. The Montessori playschool helps to improve child mental abilities, not only by limiting them to coloring and blocking buildings. They satisfy a child curiosity and help them find out what they like best. This could provide clear instructions for parents and teachers to steer their education in the right direction. Montessori schools focus on developing a child natural talent. Talent and art lessons are part of the curriculum. There is also room for physical development. Children are given play-

time in which they can develop their physical abilities through outdoor games. This can improve a child's health.

The Montessori play school introduces a child into society. Here the child learns to socialize with other children and becomes a social being. The early involvement of disciplines and methods can make them responsible citizens. The Montessori school aims to teach a child good manners and habits so that they can grow as worthy individuals. The right combination of play and study is good for the general development of your children. Research shows that Montessori education is far superior to traditional or non-Montessori schools. The principles of this form of education emphasize a safe and stimulating environment in which the child can grow at his own pace, and teachers follow the self-directed learning process.

Deep-rooted Learners

Even though much has been said about the academic accomplishments of Montessori youngsters, the worth lies in the self-authority and love of discovering that kids accomplish. Montessori schools are intended to enable every child to find and build up their exceptional gifts and potential outcomes. Youngsters learn at their pace and in ways that work best for them; the objective is to be adaptable and innovative, intending to every pulpil in a way that mirrors this way of thinking.

Montessori sets an example for a lifetime of good work propensities and awareness of other's expectations by permitting kids to build up a significant level of freedom and self-restraint. Students figure out how to invest wholeheartedly in doing things cautiously and well for the sole purpose of self-satisfaction.

Each youngster is brought into the world with an inclination to learn, with a profound love for impersonation and perseverence of deliberate work, and with one instinctive point: their self-improvement. Dr. Montessori accepted that training is a forever groundwork and should assist kids with building up a solid self-idea and an inspirational demeanor toward learning while securing the essential examination abilities which will serve them all through life.

26

CHAPTER 3

WHY MONTESSORI STYLE SPACES ARE IMPORTANT?

The following are some of the many reasons why Montessori style spaces are important.

1. Creativity

Montessori style of spaces are important in a manner that they give creativity to the mind of the toddles, and by all means, they are able to get more and more about their intellectual level. You will notice that in a Montessori style of space, the kids are able to see more bright colors and formations on the wall. They see more cartoons and depictions on it with time. They are able to garner more knowledge and ideas about things that hit the minds of the toddlers. They can receive an equal amount of courage and stamina for watching the Montessori depiction, and they will finally come in contact with the purpose of excellence for the kids. Thus, the edifice of creativity is very acceptable for the kids, and they are able to get to the most required amount of acceptance that they want from a Montessori Principle. This is the reason why you are able to induce creativity in the minds of the public due to which you are all fine and great in the coming matter. Therefore, creativity is given to your child through a Montessori style space.

2. Playing with Toys Encourages Stamina and Love for Others

Often, in a Montessori style of teaching, the toddlers play with the toys so that he can learn the art of passion and compassion for others. The toys of the children are the tactics and techniques that the child can learn more and more about life.

3. Using the Style for Activities

In the Montessori style, the places are utilized for many activities. Activities like painting, music and art play are important for the kids to learn, and they develop great skills in the kids so that people can learn more and more about it. The style is simple that the children be allowed to do whatever they want to do, and with time, they can reach the zenith of life and space. The activities are positioned at every corner of the room, and the parents are allowed to teach the child more and more about the working of the room. The first and foremost impediment to this activity can be in the form of painting and coloring. The painting and coloring can help make the kids more productive and get all the possible accessible versions of it. There is enough room in the mind of the public, and the kids can also qualify for the benefit of themselves.

The style of activities is pertinent for the kids to learn at all means necessary, and you can come up with any possible discretion to get to the best of your kids. So, the best use of these activities is to give your child a possible way to groom and evolve.

4. Montessori Style Teaches the Importance of Reflection

In a Montessori style of decoration, the child is blessed with a plethora of mirrors that are placed at many angles. They are placed at many angles so that the child can see his-self and can get to know himself coherently. The idea is that the child is not able to recognize his eyes, ears and hair or any body part by the

name of them, and as a child, it takes time for them to recognize it. However, when you have a toddler toddling on the floor, and at the moment, he reaches on the floor and looks himself in the mirror, he sees a different yet disparate himself that is apparent. He sees a different version of himself in the mirrors and he gets himself by all means. He is able to see his eyes, ears and hair and all of a sudden, he has a new friend to get acquainted with.

Therefore, the child is able to get all his ills and whims efficiently. The whims are that he sees himself and the ills are that there are wrong modes in his brain that need some change. Thus, the importance of reflection is harnessed when the Montessori style spacing is implemented at the earliest.

Prepare the Environment

When it comes to the prepared environment of Montessori, keep in mind that there's always a place for everything and everything must always be in its place. Assign one of the rooms in your home as your child's Montessori learning environment. If there are Montessori schools in your area, go ahead and visit them to have a better idea of how to arrange this room.

You may also go online and search for Montessori classroom ideas on Google or Pinterest. Either way, having a visual image of what Montessori classrooms must look like will give you a better idea of how to arrange the room you've assigned in your own home. One thing to keep in mind though, is to make sure that everything is child-sized and at your child's level so that he won't keep asking you for assistance when he wants to take something.

Plan All the Materials and Activities to Include in Your Child's Environment

After planning the environment, it's time to think about the materials and activities to place inside that environment. You can go online to search for a complete list of Montessori materials in each of the learning areas. Then you can either purchase sim-

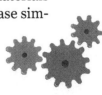

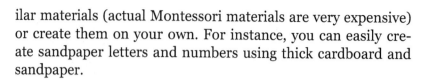

ilar materials (actual Montessori materials are very expensive) or create them on your own. For instance, you can easily create sandpaper letters and numbers using thick cardboard and sandpaper.

Arrange these materials and activities according to their areas of learning and make sure that all of them are accessible to your child. You may want to include a combination of easy materials and those which are a bit more challenging or unfamiliar to your child. Also, you may want to rotate these items regularly, so your child doesn't get bored. If you see that he's not interested in some activities or he has already mastered others and he's not using them anymore, take these materials out and replace them with new ones.

Focus on Life Skills

Activities and materials which teach life skills are the easiest ones to replicate. Children need to learn life skills early on. With these skills, they learn how to care for themselves and their environment. This sets children up to become capable and considerate adults when they grow up. Providing the proper materials to teach these skills even makes your life as a parent a lot easier! Soon, your child will start volunteering to help you around the house because he already knows how to do these chores.

Of course, you must always match the activities and materials to the abilities and age of your child. Introducing activities which are too difficult for children is never a good idea. Your child won't be able to do these activities. If you force him, this might weaken his self-confidence and his willingness to continue with the rest of the activities you've prepared.

Help Your Child Learn Concentration and Inner Motivation

These skills are essential if you want your child to get the most out of the Montessori Method. For a child to master a skill, concept, or activity, he must concentrate while doing it. If you have

prepared the environment well, your child will be able to concentrate on the activities you have prepared for him. This means that there should be no distractions such as gadgets, electronic devices, and random toys which don't have a purpose inside the room.

Also, avoid giving your child rewards when he does something good or gains proficiency in something. Try to observe your child when he realizes that he has finally been able to master a puzzle or a practical life activity. You will see a sense of accomplishment in your child. This is much more valuable than extrinsic rewards because this sense of accomplishment becomes the driving force within your child to keep on going to master the other activities in his environment.

Take on the Role of a Montessori Teacher

Finally, learning how to facilitate the Montessori Method for your child is also essential. Rather than teaching everything to your child, allow him to discover, explore, and choose the materials and activities on his own. If your child asks for help, oblige. If not, observe.

You may also step in if your child picks up material and can't figure out how to use it. Again, he will probably ask you to help him out. These are the best and most appropriate times to step in when it comes to the Montessori Method. Then when your child celebrates his mastery of a skill, celebrate with him! There's nothing more satisfying than to see your child grow, develop, and improve at his own pace and through his efforts.

Montessori is truly a wonderful learning approach. Whether it's done in school or at home, children love learning through this method mainly because of how it's done. Now that you've learned all the basics about Montessori, you may start planning how you will apply this in your home. Then step back and watch your child learn in the best possible way!

32

CHAPTER 4

A MONTESSORI PARENT: PRESENT, KIND, GENTLE LEADER

Positive Discipline from Positive and Conscious Parents

There are two types of education: the formal and the informal. Informal education is self-taught, without any help or guidance from a proper educator. The person gathers knowledge and information from their surroundings, making their self-education a priority.

Formal education comes through established institutes and teachers. These institutes cater to the children according to their ages. Kindergarten, primary or elementary school, high school, college, and universities are examples of such institutes. The roles of parents and teachers work parallel to each other.

Montessori Parents

When it comes to education, there are two ways to get educated that are formal and informal. In informal education, the person gets self-educated without any help or guideline from a proper educationist. He gathers knowledge and information from his surroundings, makes self-studies his priority. While on the other hand, formal education comes by means of proper institutes and teachers. These institutes cater to the children according to their ages. Kindergarten, primary, elementary, high school,

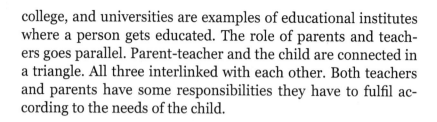

college, and universities are examples of educational institutes where a person gets educated. The role of parents and teachers goes parallel. Parent-teacher and the child are connected in a triangle. All three interlinked with each other. Both teachers and parents have some responsibilities they have to fulfil according to the needs of the child.

A Parent as a Directress

A parent has the toughest responsibility of raising a child. They are responsible for bringing the toddler into this world and addressing their needs before and after birth. Even so, a parent should acknowledge the fact that they are their child's caretaker, not their sovereign. It's their responsibility to provide a child with a safe and well-prepared environment for their potential growth.

The parent is the first formal educator in a child's life. From infancy, and throughout their lives, a parent will stand by their child's side, offering guidance as to the child's needs. Of course, we're talking about the parent as a guide, not an adult who forces their views on the child. Restraining, pressuring, and controlling the child will never yield positive results for a child or parent.

A parent should realize the difference between guided instructions and forced behavior. They should give the child enough freedom and independence to develop the confidence needed to survive in society. Letting the child make their own choices will enhance their decision-making skills in the future. They also are the judges of whether their choices were right or wrong and will eventually learn to make sensible decisions.

Parents should build a strong connection with their children so that they can learn how to build trust in others. A parent should also address their child's individual needs or wants. If the child is hyperactive, for instance, special care and a sensible approach are needed to enable them to learn better.

For this purpose, parents have to learn to become keen observ-

ers so that they can sense the needs of their children and act accordingly. They must also learn to control their temper since outbursts of anger can harm their child. If a parent displays a positive attitude, their child is sure to pick up on this and live a happier life because of it.

Your relationship with your child is just like every other relationship. For it to thrive, healthy communication is crucial. In simple terms, communication is when you send and receive information to and from another person. This information can be visual, auditory, or some other kind.

The Montessori Directress

Dr. Montessori referred to educators using her method as "directress" rather than "teacher." This is because "teacher" is a common term given to a person who teaches their students. But because within a Montessori environment, the child is learning through guided instructions, not by the traditional method of learning, the educator in charge is only offering the child guidance.

A directress is in charge of preparing a safe environment with lots of physical and mental activities for the child to explore and learn. A directress should let her presence be felt and offer instructions to the children, but never interfere or make restrictions. As mentioned before, Dr. Montessori believed that the restrictive attitude of adults could shatter a child's self-confidence.

Dr. Montessori proposed two significant roles for a directress. One is preparing the environment for the child, and the other one is the preparation of the adult as an observer and guide who knows how to prepare and take care of the child. A directress should guide children and make them spiritually strong. To accomplish this, they need to understand the child's needs.

According to Dr. Montessori, a directress is a scientist who connects with the child in a way that enables the child to explore the world around them. Instead of knowing how to teach, a direc-

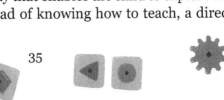

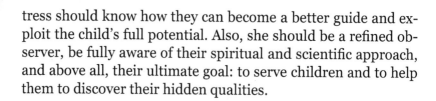

tress should know how they can become a better guide and exploit the child's full potential. Also, she should be a refined observer, be fully aware of their spiritual and scientific approach, and above all, their ultimate goal: to serve children and to help them to discover their hidden qualities.

Communication with the Child

Communication builds trust, and as such, you must get it right, especially in the early stages of your child's development. If your child feels like you understand them, it will be easier for them to relate to you and form better relationships in the future.

Healthy, open, and expressive communication with your toddler will benefit them for the rest of their lives. Everybody loves to be understood, appreciated and respected. Toddlers and children are no different. When you communicate with them often, it makes them feel you value and respect them, which boosts their self-esteem.

Parents and educators who communicate openly will often have more obedient children. When you can communicate effectively with your toddlers, they are more willing to do the things you tell them to do. They see reason in what you are telling them to do, they understand you, and do these things not only because you asked them to, but because they want to. Remember, they are independent.

Communication with toddlers can be very tricky, though. You have to know just the right things to say in the right situations and what to avoid so as not to hurt their feelings. Here are a few tips on how to tread this slippery road.

- Ask and wait for a response. A child's mind is always wandering. They could be completely absorbed in an activity one moment then run off to play the next. This is due to their need to explore anything and everything around them, so when you ask a question or give an instruction, wait for a response. When they wander off or begin to talk about something else, draw their attention back to the subject and, nicely but firmly, ask for a response.

- Children have spats with one another; it doesn't necessarily mean anyone involved is a troublemaker. Human beings and conflict are inextricable from one another. However, what you do in these situations goes a long way in the development of your child. If your child has a disagreement with another child, instead of settling the issue, guide them in resolving their problem. This instils social intelligence in everyone involved, teaching them that disagreements and misunderstandings can and should be solved by dialogue.
- It's frustrating when children refuse to share. It causes a ruckus, and it seems like there is no just way to settle it. So, Lisa wants to play with Chloe's doll, but Chloe doesn't want to share. Lisa gets hurt and begins to wail, but Chloe is set on her decision: it is her doll, after all, and she is not sharing. Instead of taking the doll from Chloe and handing it to Lisa, ask Chloe to share. If she refuses, let her be. Children are wired to think of themselves first but can be given when they want to. Find something else for Lisa to play with, then when Chloe is done, she can have the doll.
- Let your child know that you understand them when they're sad, instead of just assuming to know why to ask them about it. Prompt them to talk and listen without judging. Ask them why the situation is making them sad, then ask them what they want to do about it.
- Always ask questions. At this point, you probably already know the importance of asking your child questions instead of jumping to your conclusions. You might think you have a handle on what the problem is but hearing them talk about it will give you a fresh perspective. It also allows them to vent and express themselves. This step will also make them feel like they can talk to you about anything, no matter how big or small it is.
- Never turn a blind eye to the feelings of your child. When you have hurt them, whether you think they deserved it or not, acknowledge it and apologize. Explain why you did it and call a truce. Children are human beings with real feelings, and they are infinitely more sensitive than the average adult so that the smallest things can get to them.

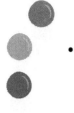

- Try not to lie to your child. The truth is children are very observant of what goes on around them and even though it may not seem like it, they know when you lie to them. The child may not call you out on your lie or contradict, but they still know.

- Use the proper words for objects. Avoid slangs as much as possible; we don't want our toddlers picking up on wrong words, right?

CHAPTER 5

A MONTESSORI CHILDREN HOME

Many parents feel overwhelmed when it comes to creating a Montessori home environment. There is a lot to take in. However, as we mentioned earlier in the guide, you are learning along with your child, and it isn't necessary to incorporate everything all at once. It's better not to do that because both you and your child may feel overwhelmed. If you have a newborn child, it will be easier to start introducing Montessori right away than if your child is a little older. Nevertheless, no matter the age of your child, they will be a great benefit and adjust quickly.

One of the many wonderful things about Montessori is that it can be applied to most settings. Even if you have a small space, you can still create Montessori at home because it's about making the most of what you have, not what you don't have. This is a perfect opportunity to get creative. Here are four ways you can implement Montessori at home regardless of how much space you have:

1. **Less is more**. When you look at other Montessori home environments on blog posts, social media, etc., you will notice that there aren't a lot of materials and the items they have are few, high quality, creative, and colorful or stimulating. This is the Montessori way. Any activities that are on display should be the ones your child is currently working with. They should be age appropriate. Remember, the younger your child is, the fewer items or toys they will need. You will need to provide some more resources once your child grows, and their skills and abilities develop—but it doesn't have to be a lot more.

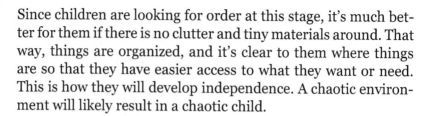

Since children are looking for order at this stage, it's much better for them if there is no clutter and tiny materials around. That way, things are organized, and it's clear to them where things are so that they have easier access to what they want or need. This is how they will develop independence. A chaotic environment will likely result in a chaotic child.

If you have a small shelf in a room that's just for your child, then that's fine. If you have no space to dedicate a whole room to a Montessori environment, then that's fine too.

2. If things don't look aesthetically pleasing to you, likely, they won't to your child either. Just remember to present materials in a way that looks appealing and will interest your child. It's a good idea to make sure that your child has their own space, but it should be a part of the family setting and not separate. When they go off to play, they shouldn't be cut off from the rest of the family.

3. Use pretty, naturally woven baskets to help you organize materials and activities. A basket or even something else that's made from wood or natural materials will help you to store the child's activities neatly, especially if they are being kept in the common area of the home along with other household items. You can easily find these at a thrift store. Your storage boxes, baskets, or trays don't have to match either. It may be pleasing to your child's eye to have them not match.

4. Focus on practical life activities.

Suiting Materials & Activities to Meet Needs

Many parents get overwhelmed with the feeling they need to have both the right amount of space and the right materials. Many people believe that if they don't have all the equipment, materials, and resources, they won't be able to apply the Montessori Methods properly. That's not the case. The purpose of Montessori at home is to involve the child in everyday activities and encourage them to feel like a valued family member who is

contributing to the home. A simple way to do this is to get them involved in practical life activities. For instance, if you have a small water bottle and a cloth, you can have your child help you wash the windows. You can even sing songs at the same time. If you are folding freshly washed laundry, why not have your child see if they can match up the socks for you? It can be as simple as that.

It's important not to force your child to do practical life activities. For instance, it's not necessary to tell your child they have to stop whatever activity they are doing to help you with the dishes. Instead, if you naturally make the practical life activities fun and exercise patience as they are learning, eventually they will want to help. Remember, children have a desire to be useful, and helping out gives them a sense of achievement. Many activities can be started before the child can even walk. For instance, they can sit down and sort laundry by color. Every child's learning needs are different. If you have more than one child, you will likely understand this as well. You know your child well and will be able to determine if an activity or certain materials are suitable for him or her.

In the beginning, you may or may not have an idea of what materials and activities your child wants or needs. However, this is where your "scientific research" will come in handy. You will quickly develop an understanding of what they require, the more you observe them. Then it will be easier to provide some of those materials.

Changing & Adapting

You will find that as your child grows, their needs, desires, preferences, and behaviors will change. This means you will be changing too. What works amazingly well in your Montessori home when the child is a new-born will need to be adjusted by the time your child grows to an infant and toddler. You must anticipate change and are open to it. Otherwise, it will hinder your child's ability to progress in daily life and develop as a person. Since children at this early age are looking for routine

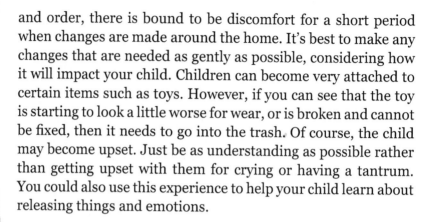

and order, there is bound to be discomfort for a short period when changes are made around the home. It's best to make any changes that are needed as gently as possible, considering how it will impact your child. Children can become very attached to certain items such as toys. However, if you can see that the toy is starting to look a little worse for wear, or is broken and cannot be fixed, then it needs to go into the trash. Of course, the child may become upset. Just be as understanding as possible rather than getting upset with them for crying or having a tantrum. You could also use this experience to help your child learn about releasing things and emotions.

You may find that your child suddenly gets bored with an activity or hates it in the first place. That's fine. Don't try to force them to do this activity if they don't like it. This goes against the Montessori approach. They may let you know verbally or non-verbally what their interests are. Remember, we want to guide children with their choices of activity. Any activities or equipment that are no longer in use can be taken out of the home. It's important to do this; otherwise, you risk your home becoming cluttered.

12 Months

- They can utilize their feet to push themselves along on ride-on toys.
- They show interest in balls and playing with them.

  » At this age, throwing or tossing the ball to your child is the key for some motor development. Begin by rolling a soft, small ball back and forth between you and your toddler, ensuring that you are gradually moving farther away. In time, they will eventually have the desire to throw it.

  » When teaching them to kick a ball, show them to use their feet instead of their hands.

  » To catch a ball, have them roll it up an incline to catch on the way down.

15 Months

- They can walk without your help, but with the assistance of walking with their feet spread apart and their arms to contribute to proper balance.
- They can get themselves up from the sitting to standing positions by utilizing their hands to push themselves up and sit down with the use of their hands.
- They can bend down to pick things up themselves.

  » In time, this action will turn into being able to squat. To assist your toddler in developing this motor skill, when they start to bend over an object, show them how to bend their knees.
  » Practice makes perfect, of course. Line up some toys and have them pick them up. This will also help in the mental development of when clean-up time is as well.

18 Months

- They can drink from a cup without assistance.
- They can draw/scribble/write on paper using a variety of utensils.
- They can climb onto low furniture.

  » Toddlers are inevitably going to attempt to climb whatever they think they can get on, blatantly because of the mere fact it is there.
  » Climbing is a vital physical development. So do not prohibit them from climbing, but rather create safe opportunities for them to do so. Throw sofa cushions on the floor and create a padded playground for them to enjoy.
  » Ensure that heavy furniture and other objects in your household, such as bookcases and televisions, are properly anchored down so that your child will not knock them over on themselves.

- They can build a tower out of block-like toys.
- They can now pick up small objects since they have practiced the pincer grip.

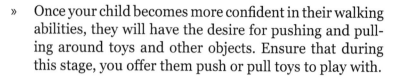

- They are able to push wheeled toys in front of them.

  » Once your child becomes more confident in their walking abilities, they will have the desire for pushing and pulling around toys and other objects. Ensure that during this stage, you offer them push or pull toys to play with.

2 Years

- They have the ability to push buttons and turn knobs.
- Most can walk down the stairs by holding onto the railing and placing both feet onto a step.
- They can easily run in one direction and stop when they need to.
- They are able to walk backwards.
- They are capable of running.

  » Each child is different, but some toddlers may go from crawling to being able to sprint at rapid rates in what seems like a matter of seconds. Some children take risks faster than others.
  » Encourage your toddler to play tag on softer areas, such as sand or grass.
  » Chase your child around, encouraging them to run from you. Then have them chase you around.

- They can get themselves off the floor without using their hands.
- They can take off articles of clothing.

2 ½ Years

- They can undress.
- They are learning ways to pick out clothes and dress properly.
- They can throw a large ball in the direction they intend.
- They can walk up the stairs.
- They can kick a large ball, even though it usually does not go in the direction they intend to.
- They can feed themselves with the utilization of a spoon.

- They can drink from a regular cup.
- They are capable of getting on and off playground equipment.
- They are able to run smoothly (and with speed).

3 Years

- They can feed by themselves using both a spoon and a fork.
- They have begun the potty-training process.

  » This is the milestone that parents look forward to maybe the most because this means no more diapers. The age at which your toddler is ready to undergo the process of properly going to the bathroom can vary greatly. Here are signs that your toddler may be ready to start the process of potty-training:

    → Looks down at diapers and grabs and pulls them off when soiled.
    → Crosses their legs or squats when they need to go.
    → Shows interest in potty-related things, such as discussing pee or poo or wants to watch you go to the bathroom.

- They are capable of throwing and catching a ball if they utilize two hands.
- They can kick a ball with more force.
- They can jump.

  » Toddlers during this stage will begin to jump off the ground or off low objects. Jumping requires bilateral coordination skills as well as the ability to utilize both sides of the body.

    → Encourage "curb hopping." Hold your toddler's hand and stand next to a curb or step and say, "One, two, three... jump!" then jump down with them.
    → Teach them to leapfrog. Demonstrate how to get down into a half-squatting position and to throw their arms up in the air while hopping.

- They can balance themselves and can walk on tippy-toes.
- They can walk both up and down the stairs without the parent's help.
- They can begin to play with ride-on toys like bicycles.

The toddler stage is quite a unique one during the course of human development in the fact that toddlers are no longer consider babies by they are not considered to be pre-schoolers yet either. There are a lot of crucial developmental components that occur during this time frame, which is why as parents should always be encouraging growth and watching for signs that our young child may be falling behind developmentally. Of course, all children learn and grow at different paces.

Gross Motor Development

Gross motor skills are physical capabilities that utilize large bodily movements that require the entire body. During the time your child is a toddler, they stop toddling and look so particularly awkward when they walk. They begin to walk and are able to do so more smoothly. They can run and at much faster rates, as well as hop and jump. They have the capability to actively participate in throwing and catching a ball and can push themselves around by themselves or while upon a riding toy.

Fine Motor Development

Fine motor movements are vastly different than gross motor skills because they require the ability to utilize precise movements to perform adequately. During the toddler stage, children can begin to create things they imagine with their own hands. They can build towers out of toy blocks, mold clay into recognizable shapes, and are more than capable of scribbling on paper with crayons or pens. They quite enjoy toys that allow them to insert specific shapes into one another. This is also the time parents will start to notice which hand their child prefers to use over the other, as they begin to become either right-handed or left-handed.

The Need for Continued Learning

You are going to find that unexpected things will come up in daily life, and you may not be sure of the best course of action. This is natural and happens with all parents. As a conscious Montessori parent, you may question your actions and choices at times, and that's fine. Please know it's important that you permit yourself to keep studying the Montessori approach because there's a lot of information to absorb.

Popular Blogs

There are many popular blogs out there that are dedicated to the topic of Montessori at home. Many of these blogs are run by parents like you, who are dedicated to raising the best human beings possible with the resources that are available to them. Many parents have made what they may call "mistakes" along the way, and they share their experiences on their blogs. You will find blogs that relate to specific concepts of the Montessori Method as well as those that discuss all the areas.

Over time, you may even decide to set up a blog yourself so that you can share your experiences with other parents and caregivers to help you on this journey further.

Ideas and Inspiration on Instagram and Pinterest

If you ever need some inspiration on how to create your environment, then Instagram and Pinterest are ideal places to visit. Many Montessori parents like to post images or create pinboards that show how their home environment is set up when the child is a newborn, infant, and toddler. As you browse through the countless photos, you'll notice that many differ from each other, which should reassure you that there is no right or wrong way to create your own Montessori environment.

There are a lot of ideas for DIY projects and activities, so if you're concerned about your budget or space, don't be. Start a

pinboard on Pinterest and save your favorite pins on Montessori ideas so you can easily refer to them. You will never be short on ideas and inspiration. If anything, this is what can overwhelm parents. However, I would like to remind you again that it's a good idea to keep it simple. If you find yourself spending hours at a time looking through Instagram posts or Pinterest boards, it may be time to look away so that you don't feel stuck. There are many beautiful home environments that others have created and seeing them can leave you feeling doubtful of what you can create. The key is not to allow yourself to get too caught up in other people's ideas that you don't believe in your own. Also, it can be very easy for many new Montessori parents to feel inadequate or disheartened because they compare themselves to what other parents are doing. The purpose of using social media is to uplift you and open you up to a wide range of possibilities for your child. It should inspire. If you find yourself feeling discouraged, then step away for a while. You will also find articles, videos, and blog posts on how to deal with feeling overwhelmed or uncertain when it comes to setting up a Montessori environment at home.

Super_Bonus Scan

CHAPTER 6

IT IS ALL ABOUT OBSERVING. THE MONTESSORI SCHEMAS FROM 0 TILL 12 MONTHS

Good Parenting

- Each baby is different.
- They need your attention.
- They need your love and care.
- Good parenting does not mean providing your child with perfect things.
- Good parenting is about giving attention and lots of love.
- Good parenting is about being nice to your child.
- It also means bringing up your child in a happy environment.
- How to monitor the growth of your baby?
- It is a good practice to keep a notebook/diary for your baby.
- A diary is like a quick reference.
- You can note step by step growth of your baby.
- You can also maintain the vaccination schedules in the same diary.
- Carry the diary whenever you visit the health center for regular check-ups.

How to Communicate with Babies?

Talk to your baby from its birth as it will start recognizing your (mother's) voice.

- Talk about what you're doing as if it is understanding.
- Sing songs and rhymes.
- Read books and tell stories to your baby from birth.
- Listen to your baby's first efforts at babbling and then respond.
- Name the toys and objects around it.

Understanding Development: Physical activities

- As your baby advances, its sleep pattern will be more defined. Between each nap there will be more gaps, note them and try to follow a pattern in feeding.
- Take out time to play with it; each member of the family can contribute to its growth and development.

Around 3 months	3-6 months	6-9 months	9-12 months
The baby tries to lift his head.	The baby tries to roll over.	The baby tries to sit & play or crawl around.	The baby tries to get up with support and try to walk.
Baby tries to lift its head to see you, tries to smile while looking at you.	Place some toys around for the baby to reach out to them.	Give the baby safe toys to play, he or she will learn to hold and play with them.	Be always watchful and alert as your baby tries to crawl or stand up and explore.

As your baby advances, its sleep pattern will be more defined.

Between each nap there will be more gaps, note them and try to follow a pattern in feeding.

- Take out time to play with it; each member of the family can contribute to its growth and development.

Social and Emotional bonding

Around 3 months	3-6 months	6-9 months	9-12 months
The baby develops trust in you.	The baby will show its feelings.	The baby reacts to familiar surroundings.	The baby enjoys playing with you.
Comfort your baby if it cries, so that he can trust you	Babies can express love and fondness just like you.	Babies hesitate to go to strangers, don't force.	Play with your kid, and they love your bonding.

Babies develop a bond with their mother, father, and siblings.

- Babies develop a bond with their surroundings as it grows.
- Babies feel safe and secured among familiar people.
- Babies may fear new faces, crowded places & new surroundings.
- Hence, talk to your baby in a soothing tone while introducing it to new people and new places.

Baby's responses

Around 3 months	3-6 months	6-9 months	9-12 months
Your baby will respond positively to your touch.	The baby tries to hold things.	The baby tries to play and learn.	The baby moves around and is inquisitive.
The baby can see objects within 13 inches from it and show excitement.	The baby learns and familiarizes with different objects with feel & touch.	Play with your baby by building blocks. Try to teach colors and shapes of the objects.	Watch her closely, as she is moving all over the place. Baby understands you tone and expression when it hears your voice.

Talk to your baby, show eye contact, and encourage it to make sounds, so that he gets familiar to everyone's voices. Baby will gradually learn to look around even when it hears a voice from a distance.

Baby knows best

Around 3 months	3-6 months	6-9 months	9-12 months
The baby knows your touch and feel.	The baby knows it's routine, hence follow one.	The baby knows to comfort itself.	The baby knows your simple commands.
Sing a song or play some rhyme while you hold your baby close.	Feed your baby, give him a bath, and put the baby to sleep at the same hour every day.	Babies can comfort themselves by holding a toy, a blanket, or by sucking thumb.	The baby can respond to you simple "NO" and "DO NOT TOUCH" commands.

If your child is crying hard, it's because this is the only way she can tell you that something is wrong.

- Maybe s/he's cold, hungry, have pooped or peed or can be in pain.
- Don't ignore your baby when she's crying as they are too small to sort it by themselves yet.

54

CHAPTER 7

IT IS ALL ABOUT OBSERVING. THE MONTESSORI SCHEMAS FROM 12 TILL 24 MONTHS

Montessori materials are an integral part of the so-called pedagogical "preparatory environment," which encourages the child to show the possibilities of his own development through initiative, corresponding to his personality.

Montessori materials in terms of clarity, structure, and logical sequence correspond to the periods of greatest susceptibility to the development of the child. These periods, which are favorable for teaching certain types of activities, identifying talents, developing self-mastery, and forming attitudes towards the world, can be optimally used with the help of developing materials.

Materials and their functions should be considered in conjunction with the vision of the child accepted by Maria Montessori, namely with his anthropology. She saw in the emerging child powerful internal creative forces that carry out the work of developing and building his personality. At the same time, the materials significantly help to streamline the child's comprehension of the world. The teacher is focused on the child with his individual and socio-emotional needs, while materials play a supporting didactic role.

For a child, Montessori materials are the key to the world around him, thanks to which he organizes and learns to realize

his chaotic and raw impressions of the world. With their help, the child grows into a culture and modern civilization. From his own experience, he learns to understand nature and navigate it. In the "preparatory environment" created according to Montessori, the child can exercise all physical and spiritual functions, shape his spiritual integrity and comprehensively develop. By organizing the preparatory environment, he learns to bring his previous experience into the system.

Sensory Development

Frames with clasps—training in specific skills needed when dressing. Children are offered frames with buttons, buttons, zippers, buckles, laces, hooks, pins, and bows.

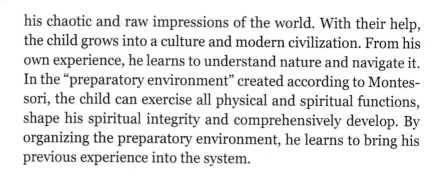

Brown Staircase—represents the differences between the two dimensions and introduces the concepts: thin, thinner, the

A   B   C

thinnest, thick, thicker, thickest.

Pink Tower—represents differences in magnitude in three dimensions and helps the child in differentiating the concepts of large, larger, largest, small, smaller, smallest.

Red bars—represents differences in size in one dimension (length) and introduce concepts: short, shorter, the shortest; long, longer, the longest.

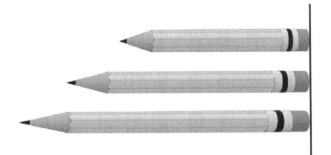

Cylinder blocks—are four sets with nine cylinders in each. The first set consists of cylinders of various heights; the second cylinders of various diameters; the other two include cylinders of different heights and diameters. Selecting a cylinder for the corresponding hole helps in distinguishing the size and developing the fine musculature of the hands necessary when writing. **Color cylinders**—each set corresponds to the size parameters of one of the sets of cylinder blocks. **Noise cylinders**—this set consists of two wooden boxes, each of which contains six cylinders. Each pair of cylinders has its own sound, i.e., for each sound of the red cylinders, the corresponding sound of the blue cylinders is selected.

Speech Development

Letters cut out of sandpaper allow the child to recognize the outline of each letter by touch and associate the sound of the letter with its outline.

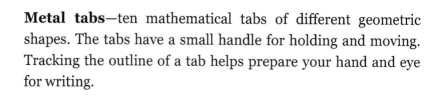

Metal tabs—ten mathematical tabs of different geometric shapes. The tabs have a small handle for holding and moving. Tracking the outline of a tab helps prepare your hand and eye for writing.

Mathematical Development

Red-blue rods are a set of 10 rods of the same size as the red rods, but each bar is divided into red-blue parts. These exercises teach the basic principles of counting and can be used to add subtraction, multiplication, and division easily.

Box with spindles—two boxes with sections from 0 to 9 are used to teach counting and the concept of quantity. The child places a certain number of spindles in the appropriate section.

Golden beads—these materials introduce the concept of counting, quantity, and basic mathematical functions.

Geometric bodies—teach visual and tactile differentiation of geometric shapes. The set consists of a cube, ball, cylinder, quadrangular pyramid, rectangular prism, ellipsoid, ovoid, cone and triangular prism.

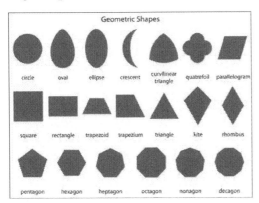

Before Buying Montessori Toys, There Are Things That You Need to Know

You want your child to become a smart, trustworthy student. But to do this, you must carefully plan the operation. No pain, no benefit, as the saying goes. You must ensure that his muscle motor is established in a healthy and uninhibited environment. You will inspire him to take on the tasks you have created. He feels safe. The learning process should be imaginative, enjoyable, and realistic in this regard.

It's important to know how children develop Montessori Toys.

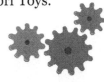

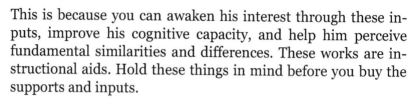

This is because you can awaken his interest through these inputs, improve his cognitive capacity, and help him perceive fundamental similarities and differences. These works are instructional aids. Hold these things in mind before you buy the supports and inputs.

1. Must Suit His Age Range

Some of the Montessori toys that help children to distinguish objects by weight may not be suited to the needs of your one-year-old kid. He's not going to understand its purpose. So, find him the ones that suit his age and interest.

2. Check the Quality

As has already been saying, playthings serve as teaching aids for learning, so that they comply with the safety parameters. But at the end of the day, you should be twice as sure as otherwise. Check the quality of the material. See how powerful it is. If screws are found, attaching one part to the other, see if they are loose, or if the color is worn out, with repeated use and application.

3. Should Encourage Creativity

Find out how it relates to your sensory experiences and experience before purchasing the content. Kids love to color, variety, and creativity, so the inputs they choose should appeal to their imagination and insight.

4. Must Make the Child Active

The chosen play should develop the child physically and psychically. While you can give him perspectives to sit and play at a corner, you also need to find things that help him understand by getting him that run, drive and leap.

5. Should Be Changeable

You will do some homework to find the correct selection of playing things that can also be used as your child matures and grows up. Find those that are modifiable and can, therefore, be used later in the next step of its growth.

Example: Doing some easy household chores like keeping his/her toys.

6. Should Motivate Learning

See whether your kid can use the product to solve a job or problem before you purchase the item. Many of the playthings like textile swats, silent games, and simple tablets help kids think critically. Find out how this piece can help your child learn and develop skills.

How Can Montessori Toys Devolve Your Children Activities?

Schooling is an important part of the life of a child in which a child establishes his personality that helps him in his life. In addition to schools, teachers, and the environment, materials, and educational equipment are also necessary. The activities and toys used help build the intelligence and power of the child. The most positive thing for children is when these toys and games are mixed.

Some of the many ways to help children learn toys and games are given here.

Better Learning Experience

Toys for education are effective in developing a child's learning experience. In addition, making children play with literature and words, many forms of educational and interactive toys are available on the market that helps them learn something new every day. Various types of fun and enticing toys help the kids concentrate on them during their activities.

Toys like alphabets, matching colors, different types of puzzles, and medleys are used to enable children to learn language fundamentals as well as math. These Montessori toys have magical powers that help them increase not only their grasping strength but also provide basics of education for various activities using toys.

Entertaining and Engaging

The available education toys are very colorful and have a quite enticing look that allows the children to be entertained. Montessori toys are magically capable of entertaining not only the children while helping them to learn, but they can also remain involved for longer periods. This helps to increase their focus and eventually boost their efficiency.

There is, therefore, a wide range of toys suitable for infants and children, in stores like Kid Advance Montessori. There are various activity toys with which the kids can take great interest and stay active for longer periods, in addition to their schooling.

Sharing and Caring

Most toys are intended for group play. It improves children's cooperation and love. Group toys help children perform the activities in a group that makes them comfortable in their company and enable them to learn the quality of time and space sharing with each other.

Simple toys are suitable for babies and children with educational programs. Such instructional and interactive toys support the child's brain. Several options such as activities, games, puzzles, lacing, and sorting toys are ideal for building a foundation for children's skills in learning, interactivity, and social competencies.

IT IS ALL ABOUT OBSERVING THE MONTESSORI SCHEMAS FROM 24 TILL 36 MONTHS

If your toddler doesn't fit the general description of the typical accomplishments, you may want to talk to your doctor, or you may want to simply back up in the book and work on the exercises for 24-month-olds. We want to make sure that your child is ready to be cared for in the ways that we describe. Your child's communication has likely exploded. They can be thoughtful, funny, and curious. They are trying on the varying shapes and sizes of independence in a thousand little ways every day. Don't be fooled. They are not adults. They do not have the same neurological capacities for logic, temper management, impulse control, and self-soothing that you do. You are still their primary source of calm, routine, and wisdom. Don't expect too little, but don't expect too much. Their combustibility is a normal part of their development. Patience is your primary parenting tool right now.

Muscles

This kid moves at a surprising clip, and no obstacle gets in their way. Am I right? At two years old, your child has far better motor control than even a few short months ago. They can climb, run, jump, stand on one foot, and kick you in the shin. Their fine

motor skills allow them to manipulate utensils and other small objects, scribble colorful pictures, and hold a cup in one hand. Their confidence and mastery in this area are but a reflection of the proficiency they feel in other areas as well.

Language and Communication

The dramatic increase of your toddler's language is exhibiting has allowed them to make meaning of other people's conversations finally, structure sentences with subjects and verbs, and sometimes hilariously, insert themselves into social relationships and communities. The gap between their expressive and receptive language is beginning to narrow. They are using language to interpret and create meaning and express their inner world. When they can't verbalize things, frustrations abound. The wonder of it all can be startling.

Social and Emotional

As new skills develop, so does the desire to exercise them. Your child's remarkable physical growth and communication prowess can cause conflict between them and their caregivers. They desire autonomy but still need limits to help them feel safe and manage the mass amount of information they take in every second. Their brains are growing quickly, and it is exhausting. Their abilities and skills have changed, and two-year-old overgeneralize this growth in all areas. They feel limitless—and the fact that they are not limitless can be a harsh reality for them.

Intelligence

Your child is entering a whole new world of play and imagination. They use their new motor skills to manipulate objects (such as trucks and dolls), tell stories, and make sense of their world. They can imitate the adults around them and mimic their routines. They are learning to interpret other people's emotions and create new ideas. Their thoughts are both practical and symbolic.

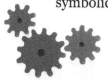

Wellness

Encouragement is a powerful tool for the development of self-esteem, but the way it is done matters quite a bit. When done well, praise is a powerful cure for hopelessness and failure. When it's done poorly, it can create feelings of helplessness in the face of challenge and reduce persistence. Since we want our children to be as resilient as possible, it is good to be intentional about the types of praise that we introduce. Compliments have two distinct variations, each of which has very different long-term implications. I want to help you build your skills in the praise process.

Proper nutrition and good sleep hygiene are important for your child. There are plenty of online resources and, from your paediatrician, to help you determine the proper parameters for these things. We will focus on social-emotional wellness by building your skills of encouragement and praise.

Learning

This is a year full of wonderful leaps and bounds in development. Your toddler is experiencing drastic growth in their expressive language, their imagination, and their abilities to problem-solve and build relationships. Learning at this stage requires patience. A two-year-old kid needs calm and present caregivers to help them name and manage their growing internal world of feelings, thoughts, and impulses.

Reading together with your toddler at any age is always a good choice. At two years old, it's transformative. Reading together at this age builds language and vocabulary, creates meaningful conversations, nurtures their critical thinking, and supports their powers of problem-solving, attention, and determination. It also provides moments for a warmth, nurturing touch. When you read with a toddler, you create opportunities outside meltdowns to discuss fantasies, fears, and challenges. You create hospitality toward emotions and demonstrate empathic atonements.

Learning Skills at This Stage

Although, social-emotional competencies are very important. I also want to provide you a checklist of skills and activities for practice during your child's second year that will round out their thinking skills and get them school-ready—even if academics aren't necessarily a priority, getting your child ready to succeed in the educational environment matters.

As you go through this list, place a checkmark beside the things that you already do regularly. Look back at the end and celebrate what a great job you are already doing.

- Encourage your toddler to scribble with markers and crayons.
- Talk with your toddler about their day at dinnertime or bedtime.
- Regularly plan opportunities for your child to interact with others their age.
- Encourage your child to use logic by seeing how they make connections. For example, "I am hungry. What should we do next?" or "It is cold outside. I wonder what we should wear"
- Use a kitchen timer to help your child learn to wait.
- Read together.
- Follow your child's line of vision and notice the things that they are seeing.
- Ask questions even if they can't answer. Wonder together about cause and effect.
- Talk with your toddler about things you are doing, especially during food preparation, driving, playing, or doing chores.
- Acknowledge and label feelings while setting limits. "I know this is your favorite toy. Still, we are not allowed to grab it from our friends. I know it is frustrating. How can I help?"
- Avoid yes or no questions. Instead, be open-ended. "Tell me about..." or "What don't you like about...?"
- Don't be afraid of tantrums. They happen. The less you react, the more quickly they can recover. Count to 10 or practice a calming technique.

- Label your child's feelings. Validation always has to come before redirection or assistance coping. A child won't accept your wisdom until they feel your care.
- Use "Pretend" play to help your child handle new or challenging situations. If you ran into a problem yesterday, act it out with dolls today and wonder about better solutions.
- Let your child lead the play.
- Encourage your child's problem-solving skills with puzzles.
- Your toddler is asking questions. Ask them what they think before you answer. Be encouraging.
- Use big challenging words around your kids. They won't always get them, but new words will create curiosity and conversation.

Boundaries and Routines

As your toddler becomes increasingly aware of their individuality and their growing powers of movement, thought, and language, are driven to assert themselves. If your child isn't occasionally expressing their likes and dislikes in demanding, angry, or rude ways—then Houston, you have a problem. These things signal healthy neurological growth, happening in the context of a healthy parent-child relationship. Further, their "upstairs brain" is at the very beginning stages of development. This means that their capacity for self-control, logic, coping, and waiting is still very small.

Families that know how to stay calm, give choices, validate feelings, and set appropriate limits have the basic skills to intervene when the children are agitated. They can prevent further upset, create a loving environment, and avoid overly frequent explosions of temper.

People often want to know what to do when their child has a tantrum. We will cover those things, too, but I always start with prevention. "I hear your family is struggling through the tyrannical demands of your toddler, but first, let's see if we can reduce the frequency of outbursts." Not only do these skills curtail the number of tantrums, but they also make de-escalation much more comfortable to accomplish.

Discipline

I know you're eager to dive into discipline. Your child can feel like a brutal jerk sometimes, and you want action. I get it. We will tackle about discipline. For toddlers, the skills that I have reviewed are the foundation for all effective control.

- Understanding their limits.
- Holding your limits.
- Expressing empathy and offering validation.
- Thoughtfully considering their behavior and trying to create solutions that teach, comfort, and prevent further escalation.

Luckily, I've been working on these things. In addition to these, your discipline at this age, which is to say your caring behavior management and teaching, should also include an ample dose of two additional things:

- Ignoring inconsequential, unwelcome behaviors.
- Selectively praising all no problematic, value-affirming behaviors.

I want to leave you with one gentler reminder:

You are the anchor in the storm. You are a teacher. You can offer natural consequences but be prepared to comfort their big emotions. Your first job is as a comforter and a teacher. Your role is not punishment. Discipline is not punishment, and you should never, ever, under any circumstances, spank or hit your child.

CHAPTER 9

HOW TO INTRODUCE AND SET UP AN ACTIVITY?

A child's mind is very absorbent; hence things impressed in mind at this stage stay with one for a lifetime. This period of education and development is referred to as a sensitive period—it is as if the child picks things, patterns, sensory and motor stimuli very effortlessly from the environment; hence this is the best phase for:

- Language acquisition: this happens effortlessly between 0 to about 6 years when the child learns sound and words so easily.
- Motor skills
- Interest in objects, based on color, shape, or size; between 18 months to 3 years of age. The child is building attention; both top to bottom attention (that is attention based on their inner decision and choice to focus on a particular detail in the environment, for example, looking for yellow color as a result of their decision to find all objects of that color) and bottom to top attention (that is interest in things in the environment that catches their attention, for example, a child's eye is caught by a yellow colored object in the environment because of how catchy the color yellow is).

Language Acquisition Activities

Books. This cuts across all ages, but the teachers tailor the books based on the life the child is living, their interests and

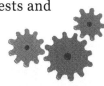

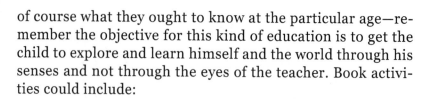

of course what they ought to know at the particular age—remember the objective for this kind of education is to get the child to explore and learn himself and the world through his senses and not through the eyes of the teacher. Book activities could include:

- One colorful picture per page for infants, so that the child can begin to take note of specific forms and begin to appreciate pictures.
- One picture per page with one word
- One picture per page with a sentence.
- Then build to making simple stories per picture.
- As you make progress, we begin to build in more complex stories.
- Get the children to arrange books in an accessible way either in a basket, or on a shelf—with this, they also learn respect for books and to order.
- For a start, a book made of the board is just fine, for handling purposes, then move on to hardcovers and then paperback books.

Rhythmic Language and Poems. This activity boosts the child's language acquisition as they begin to say words rhythmically and also, mentally match words together that seem to sound alike but have different meanings. This helps them develop a stronger grip on the language.

- Very short poems, songs, rhyming ditties; they should also be simple and be relatable for the children at their age—if they are too long, they may become very overwhelming for the children, so a few sentences or lines can do.
- Make these poems, rhymes, and songs to go with certain body movements, could be the fingers, feet, or torso—it might not be an outright dance step, you understand what I mean?
- Make these songs real and let them not be void of some emotion.

Create Activities for Self-Expression. Create avenues where the child can share something with adults or other chil-

dren. Teachers in the Montessori education system take this seriously—those moments of interaction and self-expression.

- For non-verbal children, let them make sounds and body gestures, while the teacher pays attention to understand what they are trying to communicate as well as showing emotional responses that he or she is paying attention to what the child is saying—this may demand you just restating what the child just said in your own words, repeat the sound he or she just made or just say out loud "Really!" "Wow!" "Oh My!" "Are you kidding me?" "Don't say," "You do not mean it."
- For verbal children encourage them to use words, then phrases and sentences, of course show empathy and mirror the child's emotions—do not "over-do it," making all those weird faces when what the child is saying is not that serious; children know when you are not mirroring their emotions.
- Teach the child to maintain eye contact where it is culturally acceptable, by coming down to the child's eye level and maintaining eye contact.
- A bag that contains 4 to 9 related items like cooking implements, children sized cookie cutter, spreader, bamboo whisk, spatula etc. A kimono bag filled with Japanese items, another bag filled with garden tools, hair grooming tools etc.; this would help the child learn to group things. From 2 and half years, you can start putting related things and one or two unrelated things and tell the child to spot the odd one out—apart from learning how to group things the child's register and vocabulary will expand.
- Thinking and conversation exercise; here, the goal is to get the child to think and make conversations as naturally as you can—helping the child make coherent and sensible conversations, this is for children above the age of two. You can start the conversation with "Do you remember when we planted the bean seed?" "What did we plant it with?" "Can you remember what the seed needs to grow?" "Tell me what we did as we planted the seed." This is to help the child make directed and coherent conversations with given registers as naturally as possible.

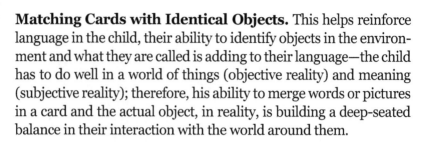

Matching Cards with Identical Objects. This helps reinforce language in the child, their ability to identify objects in the environment and what they are called is adding to their language—the child has to do well in a world of things (objective reality) and meaning (subjective reality); therefore, his ability to merge words or pictures in a card and the actual object, in reality, is building a deep-seated balance in their interaction with the world around them.

- Classifying sets of objects that match in a card or picture.
- Taking pictures of furniture or equipment that are in the right place (for example, all of these are found in the living room except _____, the child may spot that a refrigerator is not supposed to be in the living room and should be in the kitchen etc.)
- Matching identical sizes, colors and positioning.

Vocabulary Cards. Depending on the infant's age, this may come as games, wherein a child is given a picture of an object to tell its name, spelling, its uses, the application is vast, or any other form of matching such as color, size, shape, and texture.

- Set classified cards that relates to the child's everyday life and activities.
- Simple classifications where the child will talk about pictures that appear on the flashcard, this small talk can be based on anything the child knows about the picture. Of course, you will be generous with the appreciation.

Letters, Word Pronunciations and Phonetics. Cards with individual letters, two letter words, three letter words and so on as the child makes progress. From there, the child can learn those words, and other words that sound alike, spotting their differences in spellings, meaning and usage—all of these depend on the child's age and level of development.

- Flashcards with letters.
- Plastic letters in their three-dimensional form.
- Combining letters to form words.
- Identifying numbers.
- Building pre-reading skills.

Telling the Time. This is effective for children from three years and above, it helps them to appreciate better and tell the time. Provide a calendar where the child can change the day and month and also the weather; with guidance from the teacher, he can be able to communicate the date and probably the weather of the day—more details can be added later as the child grows up.

Motor Skill Activities

These are skills that help children develop muscle coordination, smooth response of the muscles when triggered by the brain, balance, poise, and grace in movement—all depending on their age and stage of development.

Music, Dance, and Movement. This helps the child make rhythmic motions, stretches calisthenics and, at the same, time enjoy music.

- Play music out loud, by that I mean it should not merely be a background song so that the children can sing and dance along.
- Videos of music and dance and the children can dance and sing along.
- Infants that cannot walk and talk yet can be placed in front of a mirror to watch their own body movements as they sway to the sound of music.

Grasping and Interlocking Materials. This helps improve their eye-hand coordination and also works on their reaching and grasping abilities.

- As the baby grows, he begins to reach out and grasp interesting materials in the environment.
- Objects placed in the child's hand can be grasped with a firm grip with a reflex grasp, but, as the child grows, he or she begins to make intentional grips.
- Ability to reach for an object, by rolling over to it, crawling towards it, or walking towards them, this can be done by placing an object of importance to the baby a little dis-

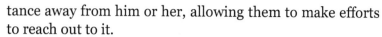

tance away from him or her, allowing them to make efforts to reach out to it.

- Toys and dolls: depending on the age of the child, he or she can use them to play, create a drama, or just bang them on the floor; all these are training motor skills.
- Place plastic or wooden interlocked rings which are able to give off sounds if rattled: children depending on their age can manipulate, mouth or throw them about.
- Hand them over bowls and scoops to scoop water or sand into a container: a distance can be created from the point of scooping to the place where they offload, to make the activity a little bit more challenging; more examples include putting plastic balls in a basket and counting them probably to know which child picked more.

Climbing Stairs with Rails. Children can be encouraged to climb platforms to perform: climb small stairs, or climb ladders to playing equipment—this helps improve their gross motor skills and their body coordination. Make stairs broad but not high and let them be fitted with rails.

Sporting Activities. This can include: running, jumping, dancing, or a combination of all to improve their motor skill and balance. These activities may or may not be competitive.

- Running down tracks with arrows for direction and filling a basket with balls: the child with the most balls wins. This helps them run, squat, reach, grasp, and throw in the right basket.
- Jumping over a flat line on the floor: once you can achieve getting a child to jump with both feet, you can now introduce elevations little by little and, of course, with a soft landing. In addition, the child can jump across slight distances.
- Riding: for about 3 years, you can introduce riding with pedals and balance wheels behind.
- Swinging: get swings that are low from where the children's feet can touch the ground so that they can swing themselves with their feet and also get on and off the swing.
- Crawling through tunnels: straight tunnels, Y shaped tun-

nels, caves etcetera, with time they may start moving and finding their way through labyrinth boxes.

- Ball swinging: throwing balls through distances, as they make progress, you can introduce targets.
- Gardening and composting: this can serve as a recreational activity for the children.

76

CHAPTER 10

MONTESSORI ACTIVITIES

List of Montessori Activities for Toddlers

Following are the list of the Montessori Activities that are exhibited in Montessori Schools that you can replicate at home.

Music and Dance

In this activity, the students or toddlers are taught to dance and respond to the audio messages positively. The parent is also allowed in this class, and the students are taught to dance while a parent is holding his hand and having fun while doing it. The child also listens to a beautiful and soft music tone that gives child momentum to move his limbs. The child is allowed to murmur beautiful songs and audible tones that reflect the inner artist of the child, and he feels very happy while he is doing it.

Reading Books

These are not big and illustrative books but are designed in a unique way to let the child understand the picture with full sheer responsibility. There is a book that has multiple pages in it, and each page has one picture in it that the child understands carefully. The picture can be of any content intended to explain the child of the nature of the content. For example, at infancy, the child is not able to understand the shape of a car, and he must be illustrated with an example. The car is a perfect example, and he can easily understand the idea of a car while looking at the picture. The same is for any other thing.

Music Box

This activity is essential for the development of the child. Still, it should be said that this activity is for the nurturing of the soul,

and it allows the students to learn things more quickly. It is a hanging box, and to activate it, children need to pull the string attached to it. This box plays a classical tone of the music of children, and the children are able to enjoy more music out of it by all means necessary. It is also used as an instrument for nap changing. The students can take napes while they pull the string and take a nap while the music is being played.

Making Stylish Papers

This activity is yet another activity that is designed to increase the visual development of the students. The toddlers are given a pack of papers, and they are shown first the art of making a fig-ure, and they are explained how to make them. For a horse, the teachers will first teach them the art of making a horse by mak-ing them cut various specimens of the paper. Then the paper will be attached so that the horse will be made and then used for proper productivity. Fishes, pinwheels and dancers are of the many examples that can be harnessed in this regard.

Making Wooden Figures

This activity creates more creativity in the minds of children. There are wooden chopped figures, and then there are pictures that are put in front of them. The children are advised to make the wooden shapes with the help of parents, and they can learn the possibilities of more inclusivity through it. There is an attractive color that is present in them in terms of more variety and vitality. Hence, the wooden figures can be used in many more designs as possible by the kids. The activity enhances the further evolutionary escapes in a child that he governs in himself with time. Therefore, this activity is more fundamental in terms of progress and productivity.

Using a Rubber Ball with Protrusions

A rubber ball gives a lot of knowledge to a young toddler, who has to learn a lot. There is a rubber ball, which is placed in the hands of the toddles, and they are allowed to do a lot of learning through it. The ball has many protrusions on it, and the child can suck on it and learn to grasp it. When the ball comes to an older toddler, the child will learn to grasp it and try to play with it. In this way, the toddler will be able to hold the ball and play it in all the possible manner and tactic. Therefore, the rubber ball has many learning aspects for the toddler and the infant; thus, the activity of using a rubber ball has many benefits for the people.

Toying With Little Balls

This activity is another mode for teaching the infants the mode of grasping other things and manoeuvring them for their good. Some balls are placed in front of the toddlers, and they are advised to play with them. Once they play, they fall and with every fall, they learn their lesson. Hence, the activity is a very inspirational mode of learning for the toddlers, and they become very bright and active while they toy with little balls.

Grasping Beads

This activity is very interesting for young toddlers to learn and they can great skills while they do so. They have to grasp the beads, and they have to make the arrangement of it strictly and cohesively. They have to identify which of the loop will come first and how they can relate it with the other character. Therefore, the grasping beads need to be arranged so that the maintainers can get the uttermost benefit of it.

Ringing a Bell on a Ribbon

The bell, which is on the ribbon, can ring many times and the children who ring them, can develop many auditory and visual developments in them. The ribbon is provided to them and they are told to ring the bell, which is attached to the ribbon at a distance. They can learn the music tone of it. Children can also come in the cognition of placement of ribbons, and they learn an important value of the bell that it is very fundamental in coming to everyone's house. Also, the ribbon is present in many colors, and those colors are used to induce a good sense of imagination in the children. Hence, this visual Montessori

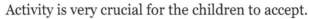

Activity is very crucial for the children to accept.

Interlocking Rings

Another Montessori activity designed for the child's visual development. This development enhances the grasping abilities of the child, and he can learn to hold things effectively. There are two or three rings that are of three colors like red, blue and green, and they can be used also to give visual development to the children. Therefore, the interlocking of rings is another Montessori activity for the individuals.

Home Objects

This activity is essential for children to bear the manipulation in the children's mind, and these are some small home objects that can be accessible by the children. These objects include honey dipper, dolly clothes, spoon, belt buckle, bangles and keys. Children are given these materials, and they are taught to hold them in their hands, through which they can learn more and more about the grouping of home materials.

Bamboo Cylinder Rattle

This is an audible educational activity that vouches to induce sounding in a child. Through it, the child can learn more and more about the voices of the bamboo, and this bamboo is used for the students to make the grounds of him more effective. The rattle is made of tinny pebbles and chains that can be sewed together and can be used for the child to learn the art of the bamboo cylinder.

Cylinder Rattle With Bells

This is a cylinder rattle with bells that is designed for the student to learn the music of the tone. This is a sanded smooth that is attached to some bells, and it is a given in the hands of a child so that he can learn the art of music from it. Some sharp bits can be used to trigger some noises in the baby, and the baby can learn a lot of new tactics through it.

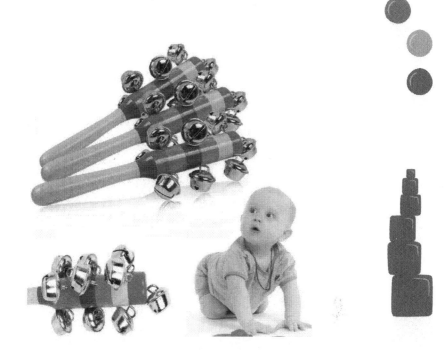

Cube With Well

The cube with the well is given to the children, so that they increase their volitional development. The development is composed of the thesis that it deals with the ability to check the motor skills and the grasping abilities of children. Also, with the cube and a ringing well in it, the children can get closer to noises and voices. These noises eventually can give more sounds to the children, and children can get more attachment to it just because they get more acquainted with it.

Bells on Leather Strap

The attached leather can help the child to bolster their holding abilities. With the Montessori philosophy in mind, they can renovate the mentality of children in a sound manner. The bells, again, give a voice development to the children to learn more about voice concerns in it.

Toying With a Suction Cup Base

For eye-hand coordination, the suction cup base is the best toy to play with. The idea behind it is very simple that the infant needs to put the toys on the suction base, and he needs to be very managerial while doing it. There are child bats, reaches and attempts that can give kids more efficacy in it and they should be able to get more perception-based approach by all means necessary. Therefore, the clever toying can help children more affectively, and they can easily reach the acme of their childish nature.

90

WRITING, READING, MUSIC AND ARITHMETIC, MOVEMENT, ARTS AND CRAFTS, LANGUAGE

Structured play is often referred to as "play with a purpose." This approach employs entertaining quiz sports, games, as well as other activities to show a learning objective as well as helping young participants develop particular abilities or know certain theories. These preschool games and also different kinds of drama are directed by instructors (or by parents, at a house setting), that help the kids meet their targets or further comprehend the training aim. Structured play isn't necessarily formal or exceptionally coordinated; tasks within this category could consist of puzzles, games, music classes, organized sports, and on occasion, maybe folding clothes.

Although you may presume that the only thing about pre-school games is having fun, organized play may foster ample chances for the child to learn and build up their abilities and their personality.

Physical Development

Through play, your child will probably grow their fine motor skills and coordination. Preschool swimming lessons, football, or maybe a form of the grab can aid your child to become better organized and produce a historical love to get physical fitness center.

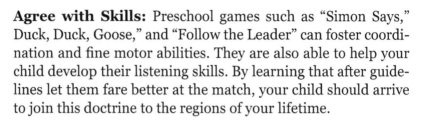

Agree with Skills: Preschool games such as "Simon Says," Duck, Duck, Goose," and "Follow the Leader" can foster coordination and fine motor abilities. They are also able to help your child develop their listening skills. By learning that after guidelines let them fare better at the match, your child should arrive to join this doctrine to the regions of your lifetime.

Social Interaction: In a conventional classroom setting, kids may not necessarily have the chance to create individual bonds together with their educators and sometimes even other students. Try to organize playdates for social interactions with children they are most close to. By boosting the significance of communicating and personalized expression in early stages, your kid will appreciate these connections all through your lifetime.

Self-confidence

Your child will understand the importance of playing with being more independent and more self-assured. That's because organized play boosts the resolution of a creative problem and critical thinking. By mastering the aims put forth with the way of a specified activity or match, your little one will come to feel a sense of achievement they can execute to other areas. Your child will continue to learn and grow through such varied tasks in a variety of approaches.

Practical Exercises

Parental involvement is vital to some of the 1-year-old's development. Really, "parents interacting with them, teaching them matters, and exposing them into age-appropriate experiences and challenges" promotes interaction and exploration.

But there's no need to pull a mountain of toys. All the whistles and bells; simple tasks also work. "I will sit with a young child with one particular block and also develop 100 distinct tasks as it's exactly about being lively and getting together using them," explains Roni Cohen Lederman, Ph.D., dean of the Mailman Segal Centre for Human Development in Nova South-eastern

University, along with co-author of both Let us Play and Learn Collectively.

Not sure how to begin? We piled several interesting Learning actions for 1-year-olds in your home.

1. Create Music

Make audio utilizing percussion tools enjoy rattles, spoons, pans and pots, bells, cymbals, and drums. "Find interesting songs to play which possess a rousing be at," suggests Dr. Myers. "Perform together with her well as inviting her to play with herself."

Skills discovered: Listening skills, Coordination, and musical quest.

2. Playhouse

Produce a fort out of a cardboard box, drama with the tube, or playhouse. Include an entry and an outlet, and invite your kid to move in and outside. You could have to reveal him first. Boost the entertainment variable with some play, such as rapping on the door or ringing the doorbell and asking if anyone's living, Dr. Myers suggests.

Skills learned: Social abilities, gross motor abilities, and investigating their environment.

3. Call a Friend

Hand a telephone for your kid and maintain you for yourself. Pretend to create forecasts and hold conversations with each other or fanciful men and women. Utilize funny voices, and make absurd characters on the opposite line. Some drama phones also permit one to capture your child's perceptions and play them straight back, which can improve the fun.

Skills discovered: Language and Social growth.

4. Utilize Water and Sand

Once your child reaches 18 weeks, fill a large bathtub with sand or water, and offer him free rein to dig, scoop, and much more. "If you are having fun with them, sing and talk together," says Dr. Myers. "Invite them to replicate everything you do, then try to replicate exactly everything they are doing." Never leave your child unattended around water. This enjoyable activity for a 1-year-old kid is especially beneficial for its creation of motor skills.

Skills heard: Creative drama, Fine motor skills, tactile stimulation, and societal development.

5. Talk Throughout a Tube

Talk via a cardboard tubing, and watch just how your baby reacts to this change from your regular voice. Let her choose a twist to find out what sounds she will create. "Children of this age want to play with speech, also this task gives them the chance to rehearse novel and new noises," Dr. Leiderman states. "Language is actually about copying sounds. Babbling turns in to real words, which turns out into a sense of humor."

Skills discovered: Auditory Discrimination, flip taking.

6. Fetch Objects

Send your kid on various "errands" around your home, requesting him to receive his shoes brings you the chunk or find his cup. Aside from practicing receptive language skills by adhering to guidelines, this learning task for 1-year-olds creates an awareness of liberty and achievement.

Skills discovered: Recognizing Instructions, memory skills.

7. Walk Contact Paper

Were they searching to get sensory activities for 12 months old? Cut a piece of contact at least 2 feet. Remove the tape and backing the touch paper, sticky side to ground, or carpet. Then make your child enjoy running, jumping, and dancing, or merely looking at the newspaper while wiggling their feet on the tacky surface. "That is a brand-new way of learning bodies," Dr. Leiderman explains. "Quite frequently, individuals as parents think we all now have to own rules for matches and do things in order. Sticky paper is only an enjoyable free for all." Parents may also put modest toys on the tacky surface and also let toddlers make an effort to pick them up.

Skills discovered: Sensory Awareness, muscle strength, human body awareness.

8. Change Her Reflection

Put a dab of red lipstick onto your own toddler's face and distract her for a few minutes before placing her in front of a mirror. If your child responds to her image by touching her nose trying to wash off the mark, then it means she realizes there is something from the standard in her expression. "Tiny kids have no feeling of ego, however in that age, it's evident for those they truly are once they try the mirror," Dr. Leiderman states. But do not worry when she does not react yet—she will soon.

Skills discovered: Self-awareness and individuality.

9. Count Fingers and Toes

Toddlers want to rely on their hands and feet, so reveal your baby just how to get each digit only once since you count out loudly. Do not worry if a kid stands outside of sequence, Dr. Leiderman states. "Children counting so isn't very important," she states. "Much like you are giving new words, amounts are a part of a lifetime. Use the context to rely on objects or feet. Therefore, they can learn the concepts of numbers finally."

For distinct variants of the learning activities for 1-year-olds, count on the staircase as you move down and up, add as you are waiting for your light to turn green, and then rely on the bubbles drifting in the atmosphere.

Skills discovered: Basic number Skills, one-of-a-kind correspondence abilities.

10. Write on Crumbs

Spread rice or crumbled crackers in a cookie sheet, and then reveal your 1-year-old how to "write" from the grinds along with his palms. "This provides kids the opportunity to mimic the adults and older sisters in their own lives, and it can be a leading purposeful activity of early youth," states Rachel Coley, occupational therapist, writer of Simple Play

.

Skills discovered: Historical Handwriting capabilities, understanding cause, and effect.

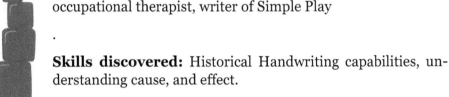

CHAPTER 12

THE TOP 10 CHALLENGES OF BEING A PARENT IN THE DIGITAL AGE

Every stage is challenging and surprising in its way. Although you will enjoy periods of relative calm and ease with parenting, you can't become too complacent. Another set of challenges awaits you at the next turn.

It's these challenges that test our resolve as parents who value a mindful approach to child-rearing. Committing to mindful parenting is one thing—acting on it is quite another, especially when you're in the trenches and trying to craft a response to your screaming banshee that doesn't involve chugging whiskey straight from the bottle and setting yourself on fire.

Over the last few decades, parenting styles and the relationship between parents and children have changed profoundly. Although parents now spend more time with their children and have closer bonds with them in adulthood, they also deal with more anxieties, guilt, and conflicting advice than their predecessors.

The clear and authoritative guidelines set by parenting experts in earlier decades (like Dr. Benjamin Spock) have given way to inconsistent messages about how much to involve yourself in your child's activities and academic endeavors. You're unsure

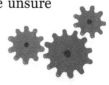

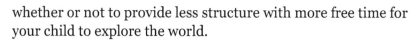

whether or not to provide less structure with more free time for your child to explore the world.

If this sounds like a depressing characterization of life for today's parents, that's not our intention. We don't mean to paint an alarming picture of your experience raising your kids. But you do have to contend with some issues unique to parenting trends over the past few decades, cultural changes related to marriage and work, and easy access to technology in virtually every corner of our lives.

Just so you're completely clear about what you're up against, let's review the top ten challenges parents face in this complex Information Age.

Challenge 1: Lack of Time

Most moms and dads today work full-time jobs with dual incomes. As a result, parenting has become a juggling act in which you're struggling to balance conflicting demands on your time and energy.

Parents don't have enough time for self-care because when they are home, they feel they should spend every minute engaged with their children. This lack of time leaves parents feeling guilty, exhausted, stressed out, and worried they aren't doing anything well. Maybe you can relate.

Challenge 2: Emotional Demands

Whether they are infants, teenagers, or any age in between, your children will frequently exert their emotional needs and make emotional demands on you that feel overwhelming.

Some of these emotional reactions relate to cultural changes children face today with ever-present digital devices, little free time or time spent outdoors, and increasing pressure to perform at school and with extracurricular activities.

Behaviors like temper tantrums, whining, arguing, back-talking,

and insults will test you to your limits. As hard as you try to stay calm and composed when your child has an emotional outburst, you will often feel at a loss for how to best respond.

Sometimes your child's emotional demands will trigger strong emotions in you that you can't control. You may lose your temper, say things you regret or inflict knee-jerk punishments that aren't well-considered. All of this adds to the emotional turmoil in your home.

Challenge 3: Aggression

When your child gets emotionally flooded, his or her feelings may come out in aggressive behaviors, especially if he or she regularly witnesses aggression in others.

Hitting you or other children, being destructive, kicking, exhibiting intense anger, and picking fights are behaviors that can trigger your own fight-or-flight responses if you don't know how to handle your child's intensity.

Challenge 4: Judgment from Others

Family members, friends, and parenting experts all have opinions about the "right" way to raise your kids. You may have people in your life who believe they're helping you by telling you what you're doing wrong and how you need to change.

Comments like, "Why aren't you breastfeeding?" or "In my day, we'd let the baby cry it out," can make you feel defensive and doubt your own judgment.

In addition, social media can be another guilt- or shame-inducing forum when you see other parents (and their "superstar" children) who feel the need to share their parenting doctrines and why they are more successful than all of the other loser parents out there.

Feelings of judgment and peer pressure can cause you to feel insecure about your parenting, and may even compel you to send

mixed messages to your children—something they will pick up on and use to their advantage.

Challenge 5: Seeking Perfection

Judgment from others on your parenting is bad enough. Still, self-judgment can erode your confidence and undermine the joy of being a mom or dad.

You may have a vision of what it means to be a "perfect" parent, and when you fall short of that vision, you feel like a failure—like you've failed your child.

Previous generations of parents didn't feel as responsible for their children's success, self-esteem, and happiness. But you want to protect your kids from pain, failure, disappointment, and heartache.

As a result, today's children don't often encounter the natural consequences, challenges, and setbacks that are an important part of learning and becoming a self-sufficient adult.

Challenge 6: Technology and Screen Time

Constant connectivity through computers, television, electronic games, and cell phones is creating a generation of children who can't disconnect from the digital world.

As a parent, you're torn between the convenience of these modern-day, child entertainment (and babysitting) devices and the knowledge that too much time on them can cause a host of issues, including attention deficit disorder, learning problems, anxiety and depression, and speech or language delays, according to research.

There's so much pressure from peers, television, and social media, that trying to manage your child's digital time feels like an uphill battle.

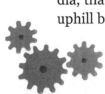

Challenge 7: Over-Scheduling

Today's parents feel less comfortable than previous generations of parents allowing their children the untethered freedom to play outside and roam short distances away from home on their bikes. There are too many real and imagined dangers to allow that kind of autonomy.

Parents are also more performance-focused and worry that their child won't survive in our competitive economy if Mom and Dad don't intervene early and often.

As a result, parents invest more and more time (and money) into arranged playdates, enrichment classes, and extracurricular activities to ensure their children have every advantage.

But this overscheduling creates more stress and pressure for both parents and children and doesn't allow kids just to be kids. Many high-achieving young adults are suffering from anxiety, depression, and other mental illnesses in an effort to rise to parental and self-expectations.

Challenge 8: Not Listening

One of the most common complaints you hear from parents is that their children don't listen. Getting your kids to pay attention and follow instructions feels like herding fleas.

Often, you repeat the same request a dozen times before it sinks in (or it's acknowledged), and your child takes action. You resort to nagging or yelling to get his or her attention, but then you feel guilty and bad about yourself for losing your temper.

The old rule, "I'm just going to say this once…" no longer applies. Your child is too distracted or doesn't fear the consequences, and therefore tunes you out. You feel conflicted and out of control.

Challenge 9: Letting Go

As your child gets older, it's natural that he or she will gain more and more independence and accept more personal responsibil-

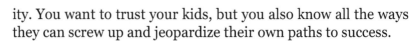

ity. You want to trust your kids, but you also know all the ways they can screw up and jeopardize their own paths to success.

You want to protect your children from harm, poor decisions, and mistakes, but if you want them to learn valuable life lessons, you must let go and allow them to "fail forward" if necessary.

Many parents find this process the most challenging of all, as they have invested so much time and energy into their children that it's hard to bear the thought of their children squandering their efforts with one bad decision.

Challenge 10: Failure to Launch

There is an epidemic of young adult children who "fail to launch," still living at home or depending on parents emotionally and financially long after they should be self-sufficient and managing adult responsibilities.

You may not be worried about this challenge now, when your child hasn't even reached their teen years, but it's wise to recognize this problem is real. It's never too early to teach your kids the practical skills they need to become independent adults—beginning with natural consequences, personal responsibility, and saving money.

As a result of creating child-centered environments at home or protecting their kids from consequences, parents can find themselves in the untenable position of pushing their child out of the nest rather than watching them fly away with ease.

Because we remove obstacles from our children's lives and do backflips to ensure their happiness during childhood, young adults often don't have the coping skills to face real-world challenges. As they flounder, you are left wondering, "What did I do wrong? I gave them everything!"

CHAPTER 13

LET'S TALK ABOUT DISCIPLINE

Discipline means to teach no punishment, but it also means solid clear limits and consequences for behaviors that are or can be dangerous (play with knives or sharp objects/ crossing the road, pushing others, etc.). For long-lasting behavior change.

The beginning of all effective discipline is parental self-control, thoughtfulness, and intention. At 12 to 18 months, when a child's ability to inhibit their behavior has not yet developed, there is no real necessity to discipline them for any reason. You can express boundaries and celebrate target behaviors—but scolding them for developmentally appropriate behaviors like wandering and mess-making should not be something a parent does at this stage. It is appropriate to prohibit certain behaviors by offering simple course correction or redirection, but anger about your child's poor self-control should be off the table.

Remember, discipline is much closer to the word "discipleship" than it is punishment. And yet, punishment is the word most parents closely associate with discipline. From zero to three years of age, it is especially important that we make sure all our discipline is rooted in teaching, connection, and care. During this time, while your child might be coloring on the walls and throwing food on the floor, make connection priority. Always share your expectations for their behavior in a way that expresses a benevolent understanding of both their limitations and their desires.

Effective Discipline vs. Punishment

Punishment has a punitive nature and does not change the behavior of a child. In many cases, punishment can even make the situation worse. The child only suffers and learns nothing. Unfortunately, punishment also tends to subject the child to humiliation, serious discomfort, anger, more frustrations, and anxiety, among others. On the other hand, effective discipline is both safe and healthy for the child. Although punishments are also used in an effective discipline strategy, such punishments are mild and only play a part of the whole strategy. Last but not the least, punishment controls a child while discipline guides a child, allowing him to learn from his mistakes and grow beautifully.

Say No to Spanking

Although spanking can be traced back to ancient times as a way to discipline a child, various studies today show that it is not effective. In fact, spanking can even make the situation worse. Spanking a toddler tends to make the child more aggressive, and it does not teach him the right conduct.

Spanking is based on pain. The theory behind it is that a person would not continue doing something that harms him. For example, if you touch a hot stove with your bare hands, you will get hurt, remove your hands immediately, and would no longer dare to do the same action again. Although this sounds logical enough, disciplining a child is not as simple as avoiding getting burned by a hot stove. When you discipline a child, you have not just tell the child what not to do but also what to do. Discipline teaches a toddler positive behaviors, which leads him to take positive actions.

Another thing that makes spanking harmful is that the child tends to lose trust in his parents. Your toddler looks up to you for support, comfort, and care. If you become a source of pain to them, especially if it happens a lot of times, then your child would tend to step back and put a shield around himself. This naturally damages the parent-child relationship.

If you are a parent who is used to spanking your child probably because that was how you were "disciplined" when you were young, or maybe because you simply thought it was the best way to save from child from being a bad person, here are five ways that you can do to stop yourself from spanking your child and be a better parent.

Learn to Use Words

Use words instead of physical aggression. Control yourself and talk calmly without scolding, and be sure to use words that your child can understand. Toddlers have a short attention span and cannot analyze things as good as adults, so keep your words short and simple. Since you communicate with words, you must also listen to your child. It should be a two-way conversation so that there will be understanding. It is also likely that there will be fewer problems if your child feels that you are listening to him. Just as you get exasperated when you feel that your child cannot understand what you are saying, your child also feels terrible when you do not listen to him.

Shift of Focus

Many times, all it takes is a shift of focus. Instead of focusing too much on the negative, focus on the positive behaviors. By giving all the time to positive things, there is no opportunity for the negative behaviors to even manifest themselves.

Let Him Learn On His Own

As people always say, "Experience is the best teacher." This is also true for toddlers. There are times that you do not have to spank your child just for him to learn. By simply letting the normal flow of things to unfold by itself, your toddler can learn from his own actions. For example, if he continues to play with his toy despite your warning roughly, the toy can soon break. This will teach your toddler a good lesson, which is more effective than simply spanking and hurting your child. But, of course, if there is a risk that is threatening to the life and well-being of

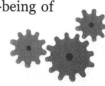

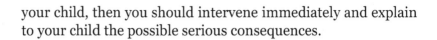

your child, then you should intervene immediately and explain to your child the possible serious consequences.

Take a Timeout

Take a timeout. Except that this time, you should be the one who should take the timeout. Just before you lose your cool, give yourself a break. Step back for a minute and cool your temper. It is important to note that you should not face your toddler when you are not calm and centered. Unfortunately, if you are in a public place and you cannot step back and leave your kid alone, the best thing you can do is to pray and think of happy thoughts.

Have the Realization That Spanking Does Not Help

Time and again, various studies show that spanking is not a good way to discipline a child. In fact, spanking can only make things worse, and it does not make you a good parent. Therefore, instead of spanking your child, think of more ways that are positive and constructive on how you can correct the wrong behavior.

Four Pillars of Effective Discipline

The most effective techniques to discipline a child are characterized by four factors, which make them not only effective but also safe and healthy for the child. Unlike punishment, the four pillars of effective discipline promote childhood learning and welfare.

1. It builds a positive parent-child relationship

An effective discipline should be supportive of the relationship between the parent and the child. Unlike punishments that are based on fear, effective discipline is based on understanding, love, and support. You should keep in mind that toddlers are very sensitive, and their early childhood relationships have a great influence on their brain development, as well as on their

behavior. By building up a positive relationship with your toddler, he will not only learn the right conduct but also enjoy a strong bond of love and trust with you.

2. **It is safe**

The safety of the child is of utmost importance. This is another reason why smart parents frown upon the use of punishments that involve bodily harm. Sometimes, the punishments can turn into cruelty and no longer serve the best interest of the child. Not to mention, many of such serious punishments are inflicted when the parent has already lost his patience and control of the situation.

3. **It has reasonable expectations**

Discipline teaches the child the right and proper conduct. Therefore, you should also consider the age and brain development of your child in making your expectations. Positive behaviors should be continuously enforced, while negative behaviors should be suppressed as early as possible. Be sure to take notice every time your child demonstrates good behavior, or at least try to do so.

4. **It is composed of multiple techniques that are safe for the child**

Effective discipline is a system of techniques or strategies. A certain technique is used depending on the situation. And, again, this pillar highlights the importance of the child's safety. Every challenging behavior should be taken as a learning opportunity, which can allow the child to learn and grow. As a parent, you must be able to approach the problem directly in a calm manner.

Is it Too late?

Some people think that it is too late to exercise discipline and that their toddlers can no longer change. It is worth noting that toddlers experience rapid changes. In fact, change is part of being a toddler. Either you turn a bad behavior into a good be-

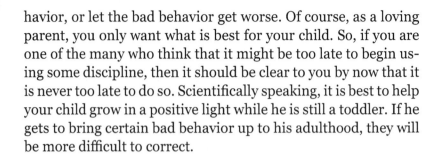

havior, or let the bad behavior get worse. Of course, as a loving parent, you only want what is best for your child. So, if you are one of the many who think that it might be too late to begin using some discipline, then it should be clear to you by now that it is never too late to do so. Scientifically speaking, it is best to help your child grow in a positive light while he is still a toddler. If he gets to bring certain bad behavior up to his adulthood, they will be more difficult to correct.

What if It Does Not Work?

Another common dilemma shared by most parents is what if nothing changes even if they try to discipline their child? There are certain points to consider. First, there are many techniques that you can use to discipline your child. Second, you would not know if it will work unless you take the action to do so. Third, changing a bad or inappropriate behavior takes time and effort. Fourth, toddlers usually have more than a single behavior that you should try to improve. By applying a form of effective discipline, you can at least help him change some of his bad behaviors. If you are lucky enough, you might put right all his inappropriate manners. Fifth, exercising discipline increases the chances that your child will grow as a good person. Sixth, change happens not only in toddlers but also in adults. Therefore, there is no good reason to think that you cannot change your child's behavior. At the least, you can be able to teach him some good manners. Last but not the least, it is your responsibility as a parent to do everything for your child, to make him grow the best way you can.

All kids need boundaries. Boundaries are not only a great way to teach your toddler good behavior, but they also help him feel safe and secure. The tricky part about boundaries is setting and enforcing them. This becomes a little difficult, especially if you want to avoid bribing, threatening, or coercing your child to listen to you. You must be calm and set firm limits for your child. This is a simple exercise you must repeat time and again, without any inconsistencies. There are no timeouts when it comes to parenting - you are in it for the long haul.

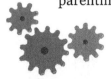

CHAPTER 14

THE COMMANDMENTS OF TODDLER DISCIPLINE

Disciplining an elementary school kid is very different from when you try to do the same for a toddler. The older kid understands language, and they know the rules. They know that mummy or daddy said we should not touch the TV because it may fall and break, and that means we shall have nowhere to watch cartoons. A toddler wonders why they cannot touch that beautiful screen and probably thinks that you are mean—or that they are being kept from the fun stuff.

Does it mean that you let them off the hook probably because you think that they are too young to understand rules and consequences? Not! You want to bring up a good world citizen and a member of your family, don't you? Then do not spare that toddler; teach them to do right.

However:

Discipline for a toddler is quite a touchy issue, and every parent who has succeeded in raising well-mannered and intelligent children has had to learn the following commandments—mostly the hard way. In the practical ways to deal with behavior and emotional challenges, you will notice that the solutions to these issues rely on the commandments below. Observe them as you discipline your child, and you are likely to have an easy time and successfully achieved the desired results.

Statements Must Be Short and Sweet

Their little minds cannot comprehend long sentences. For this reason, you find that they only understand short statements. For instance, they will understand "come here," "no biting," "stop," "no," "no touching."

However, if you go for "Liam, you know it's not good to bite your friends" or "Mandy, you need to stop pulling on the cable." Trust me; you will lose Liam right after "you know" and Mandy at "you need." Just say "Liam, no biting," or "Mandy, stop pulling."

Please, No Yelling

The loudest voice you can use may stop your child from doing whatever—or not, especially when it becomes a habit. However, it signals that you are losing control—of yourself and the situation, and your lovely child may get scared of your voice, but they are not going to respect.

All of us yell at times, but you realize that at those moments, you are not feeling in control—and that little one notices it too. Do not be surprised when they assume your instruction when you yell.

Do not yell. What you do is change your voice. Understand that it's not the volume, but the tone of your voice that communicates and gets the points across. Remember how that soft-spoken teacher was the most respected—and most strict? You probably had a funny name for the yelling one you never listened to—you do not want to be this one.

Therefore, you may want to focus more on tone and keep your volume normal when instructing a toddler.

Act Immediately—on the Spot

They do not have a long-term memory to remember what they did and also, they do not have the mental capacity to connect previous action and present consequences.

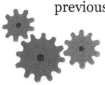

If your child is doing something wrong, you should never post-pone serving the consequences. If they need to be disciplined, it has to be done right on the spot of action. Do not wait because five minutes later, s/he will be onto something else, and they won't remember what wrong they did to deserve punishment.

Do not Make Promises as 'Pay' for Good Behavior

"If you eat your food, I'll buy you chocolate," "if you are nice to your friends, I'll get you that toy you want" it works, doesn't? They will do what you want to get that reward—no arguments or rebellion. Phew!

It's easy and that's why it's very tempting. Do not do it. It's true you will get them to behave, especially when you offer something they love. However, what you will have succeeded in doing is to bring up a two or three-year-old who knows that any good behavior has a price tag. You do not want your child to turn out manipulative or corrupt, do you?

Choose What Battles Are Worth Fighting

You do not want to fight with your child every time over every little thing they do. They will assume that you are always fighting or saying "no" and won't pay attention to your correction. For instance, if you say "don't touch" 25 times a day, eventually, it will lose its effectiveness—and they will touch.

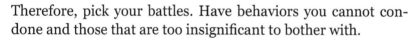

Therefore, pick your battles. Have behaviors you cannot condone and those that are too insignificant to bother with.

For instance, if they scream every time you pick a call, just ignore them. Eventually, they will know that they will not get a reaction out of you and drop the behavior.

Condemn the Behavior, Not the Child

You love your child, don't you? You want to raise a child who knows that their parent loves them. However, we sometimes

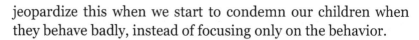

jeopardize this when we start to condemn our children when they behave badly, instead of focusing only on the behavior.

Always tell them that a particular behavior s bad; never tell them that they are bad. Tell them that what they did was something foolish, but do not tell them that they are fool. This is the best way to communicate, "I love you, but I do not love the way you are acting right now" or "you are smart, but what you are doing isn't that smart."

Correct, Redirect, Repeat

When with a toddler around the house, you'll probably do this all day. You will catch them doing something they shouldn't, tell them "no," and attempt to distract them with a different activity. Chances are, they will try to go back to the previous "wrong activity," which they find to be entertaining for some reason and see if they can get away with it.

It can be frustrating, but if you want to etch the "I should not do this" memory in their little brain, you should not give up. Correct, redirect and repeat even if they have returned to that activity for the tenth time.

There Shall Be Consequences for Actions

Teach your child that there are outcomes for their behavior. They need to understand that actions come with consequences—a lesson that will be of great help in their adult life.

Some consequences include missing out on activities they love, the time-out corner and so on. For instance, if they bite or hit their friends while playing, they ought to know that it will automatically earn them some time in the time-out corner, alone and with no one to play.

Note: missing out on your love should never be a consequence. Do not push them away or refuse to cuddle, comfort or be there for them when they genuinely need you as punishment.

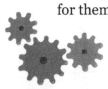

You Shall Not Back Down or Compromise to Avoid Conflict

Sometimes it's tempting to let them have their way, especially when they roll, scream and kick in a public place, and everyone is giving you the "give them what they want so they can shut up" look.

If you want to reinforce or discourage certain behavior, you will need to be consistent in the direction you give your child. There shouldn't be times you allow them to do something you do not want them doing just to prevent a meltdown. For instance, if you said they cannot have candy, stick to your guns even when in a supermarket, and they are standing right in front of it screaming their lungs out.

You see, the message you want to send them is, "you cannot have candy," not "you cannot have candy, but you can grab all you want if you scream loud enough." Remember, toddlers are experts at studying your game, and they will know what drives you to give in—they will do it all the time.

Always Give Them Choices

Make your child feel important and in control by giving them a chance to choose. You do not want to raise a child, who knows only to be dominated, never being able to make their choices, do you?

However, there shouldn't be many options to choose from, as this may confuse the child. Also, they should include the things you want to accomplish. For instance say, "It's your choice: You can put on that dress or this one."

Be a Reflection of What You Want to See with Your Child

Kids do not do what they are instructed to do. They are most likely to learn their behavior and communication skills from

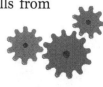

their environment. You are their first contact with the world, and therefore, they will learn from you. That kid you think to be too little to see and understand is observing your every move. They are learning how to handle situations and how to talk by watching you

.

Therefore, you have to model the values you want your child to adopt. If you do not want them to talk back, don't talk back to other adults or them, if you don't want them to complain, stop complaining about the weather or the electricity. Do not tell them what you want them to do or become, show them.

CHAPTER 15

HOW TO COACH SIBLINGS' RELATIONSHIP AND RIVALRY

Fights with Siblings

Siblings fighting with each other is another day-to-day experience a parent should expect. Fights can happen for literally any reason at all; kids can fight over toys, kids can fight for space, fights can even occur over who sits on daddy's lap, whatever it is, kids can fight over it.

Fights, sometimes, can be intentionally sparked by one child or the other; children can seek attention by any means possible, even if it is negative, and after all, half bread is better than none. Competition is another reason why siblings fight each other; fights can happen over who does what first, first to have a bath, who gets dressed first, until the end of the world, kids will compete and fight for supremacy. In the twinkle of an eye, playtime can turn into wartime between siblings.

Having a younger sibling can be frustrating for a toddler, which would cause them to express their anger by trying to start a fight. A toddler is yet to understand what it means to have a younger one; all he knows is that one new little creature has come to hijack all the attention, love, and care he's been getting.

It's not an easy job for a parent who, by the addition of a new member into the family, now has to add refereeing to the long list of parental tasks. In fact, some parents find it hard to the

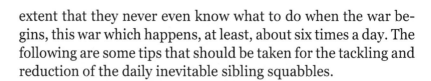

extent that they never even know what to do when the war begins, this war which happens, at least, about six times a day. The following are some tips that should be taken for the tackling and reduction of the daily inevitable sibling squabbles.

- Kids learn from what they see: Make sure you are not just telling your kids to do as you say, behave how you want them to copy; when your kids see that you handle everything that comes your way aggressively, you are only teaching them to be aggressive as well, how they see you treat and relate to people matters a lot, the kind of relationship they notice between you and your partner is another example they will learn from.

- Calmness in intervention: When fights erupt, and you want to intervene, be sure to show a high level of calmness; yelling never solves anything; it only brings about escalation; I know it is really annoying to see your kids getting in a brawl, but be sure to suppress your anger and not show your frustration.

- Try not to judge and take sides: When you hear your kids fighting over something (probably a toy), and you get there, with or without an idea of who had it first, try settling the fight regardless, putting blames can build grudges in the Kids' minds. It's normal to think about fairness, but trust me; the other kid will have the fault too some other time; there you have your balance.

- Ignorance: This will be needed at some point, when you find out that your kids start to fight in search of attention, then some amount of ignorance will help make them know that negative attention is not a way of life, because if they are always getting it anytime they fight, then they will keep on doing it anytime attention is needed. Well, a great way to prevent this is to make sure kids have a lot of equal time and attention.

- Assurance of importance: This is for an older toddler who is having a younger sibling, they believe that with the arrival of the new little one, their significance goes down the drain, they will do almost anything to make sure that doesn't happen; they'll fight for their right. This also requires a lot of attention to the older toddlers so that they can feel secure and not feel threatened by the arrival of the new one. Parents can prevent this by preparing the kid for the new baby, you create a connection even before the baby is born, having them talk to the baby, feel the baby kick, see images of the baby in the belly, can create the desired connection, making them through pictures of their baby days can also help prepare them for what is coming.

- Verbal lessons: Try explaining to your kids how bad it is to fight their siblings, show them how they can live together in peace and harmony; you can even encourage them to employ turn-taking; it helps reduce the rate of fighting as they know they will have their turns.

Fights Over the Table

Your toddler frequently gives you a hard time each mealtime; this can happen as a result of a variety of reasons. Below is a list of possible causes of toddlers' mealtime fight and their respective solutions.

- You show too much attention. When you concentrate too much on your kid at mealtime, showing too much concern about how much they eat, showing excitement when they eat well, or displeasure when they eat less. It puts pressure on them, which displeases them, and in turn, they lose interest, then the war begins.
- You can give them some amount of freedom and a sense of independence at mealtime. When they feel they are in control, then they don't get to feel that eating is an obligation.
- Transition problem. You have to work the transition into them before time; notifying them beforehand is essential so that when the time finally comes, they will be prepared. For example, when it's about ten minutes before mealtime, you say to them, "Amber, you have eight minutes until mealtime, you'll need the two minutes extra time.
- Tiredness. Kids, after so much unrest, become too tired to

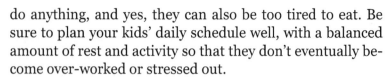

do anything, and yes, they can also be too tired to eat. Be sure to plan your kids' daily schedule well, with a balanced amount of rest and activity so that they don't eventually become over-worked or stressed out.

- Snack, eaten too close to mealtime. When your kid has a satisfying snack too close to mealtime, he becomes filled up, and digestion has not yet fully taken place when it is time for the meal, he, of course, would refuse to eat. Be sure to give snacks further from mealtime; there should be at least two hours interval between the snack and mealtimes.
- Taste disorders. Your kid might be having a condition of taste disorder, which can change how some foods taste. A specialist (pediatrician) should be consulted ASAP.

Helping Parents

When we think "toddlers," what comes after is "play," especially when we are busy, maybe doing some house chore or the other, we never believe our toddlers can be of help. Parents need to learn to understand their kids (even though it's easier to say than to execute); we also need to understand that toddlers too, apart from tantrums and other displays of anger, can be serious at times. When they see us doing some things, they also want to try, but parents always think otherwise. Sometimes, when we even recognize their willingness to help, we simply refuse and tell them, "no, you'll get to help when you're bigger." We also just prefer to do these things by ourselves just because, if we allow them to do it, they end up messing it up; It is true toddlers aren't yet perfect at doing these things, but stopping them from trying doesn't help either. Allowing kids to help in house chores aids in their growth and development into adults.

Benefits

Below are some good returns of allowing toddlers to help with tasks.

- Sense of belonging: When kids get involved in doing the household chores, they get the feeling that they, too, are recognized as an important part of the family.

- Confidence builder: Being allowed to a part in the house chores make them know that you have trust in their abilities (no matter how tiny it might seem); this, therefore, gives them a level of confidence, which eventually becomes part and parcel of their personality.
- Enhances their cooperation with others: Working together with your toddlers in doing house chores helps build their collaboration and cooperation skills. Working with other people won't be hard for them since it's what they've been doing since toddler-age.
- Promotes an appreciative spirit: When kids get appreciated for helping, they grow to become appreciative beings, since you are their role model.
- Builds self-discipline: Self-discipline and responsibility-taking are also portrayed by kids who are involved in carrying out house chores.

However, with all these being listed, it's not all kids that want to help at all time, and getting them involved when they are not interested initially can be exhausting, but they can be left alone because toddlers need to be taught to help with house chores for their personality's sake, so some tips have been developed in order to get them to help.

Tips for getting toddlers to help

- Not by force: As I have always said, kids, like adults, never like being bossed around or dictated to; there is no room for dictatorship if you want to get them to help out with house chores or other things, let them decide they want to, when they are forced, there is a very high tendency for refusal.
- Encourage collaborative work: Do not make tasks like clothes folding personal; instead of asking them to fold their own clothes while you fold yours, you can just allow them to fold anyone.
- Expect and allow the mess. It is true that help from toddlers can make things a little slower, sloppier and messy, but you have to learn to allow for the mess to happen; although you will take care of it, it shouldn't be immediately, so as to not give your kid the wrong impression.

- No task is too small: Be sure to expose your kid to every possible chore, give a wide range of tasks from helping while sweeping, to helping out in the garden, to helping with laundry and dishes. Do not limit their exploration; try and make them redirect their energy usage from throwing things, hitting, and all that show of power, into using it for useful work for the family.

- Sense of contribution: The chores you let them do, of course, can't be "big," but be sure that the tiny ones they do are significantly important that it gives them the impression that they are truly contributing.

Kids also develop gross and fine motor skills when they carry out certain tasks (with parents' help, of course), involvement in chores also help sharpen Kids' brain, which helps improve their problem-solving skills.

CHAPTER 16

RULES FOR PARENTING WITH GENTLE AND LOVE

any unwanted behaviors are caused by primary needs that only need to be met so that the child can move on to what he or she needs or wants to do. Before you complain about a child being whiny or irritable, pause and think. Is the child hungry? Thirsty? Too hot? Too cold? Sleepy? Tired? Did the child skip a nap? Is the child overwhelmed by noise or too many strangers in his face? Is her coat itchy or her leggings too tight? Is the child in need of attention?

Make Sure That Your Needs Are Met

We get grumpy and angry much, much faster when we are in some kind of physical discomfort. This can mean that you need a bite to eat, a bathroom break, a massage, a nap, or a quick shower. Whatever it is, make sure you get it. You'll be a better, calmer parent after.

Create a Child-Friendly Environment

Too often, children get blamed for things that were not primarily their fault. That vase would not have broken if you had kept it on a high shelf. Tiny champers would not have ruined that book if you had saved it for when the child is older. The dog wouldn't be neglected if you had made sure that Robert understood the concept of responsibility before you bought it for him.

Acknowledge Their Feelings

"That must have been embarrassing." "That must have come as quite a shock." "You're angry at Conrad." Even when a child's reaction seems illogical, her feelings are real to her. Show empathy by giving your child's feeling a name. This shows the child that you are on her side while also teaching her how to identify and acknowledge her own emotions.

Validate Their Feelings

Children are only just beginning to experience and understand their own emotions. Help them understand that their feelings are valid and that they won't (or shouldn't) be judged for showing any kind of emotion by saying things like "that made me sad too when I was little" or "I still get scared of the dark sometimes."

Breathe.

Try to Decipher the Underlying Cause

If you merely act on the outward behavior, the underlying unmet need will continue to surface until it is finally met. Think about the cause of the child's behavior instead of just responding to the behavior itself. Try asking questions such as "Are you mad because I got home late and we didn't get to play together? Do you think we can do it after dinner?" or "Are you sad because your sister is at camp? Do you think we should go to the park so you can play with your friends instead?"

Give Yourself Time

Count to ten (slowly, silently) before you respond. This is especially helpful for parents who have a tendency to react immediately and forcefully. It also helps to say something like, "Give me a minute. I need to think this over."

Give the Children Time

Another good way to teach children autonomy is to give them a little space and grace to figure out what they should do and whether or not they are ready to cooperate. Statements such as "Let me know when you're ready to share" or "I'll be waiting here until you're ready for a story" give children a sense of control while avoiding confrontation. Take care not to say these in a sarcastic or exasperated tone. Of course, these won't always be appropriate (particularly when you're in a hurry to get somewhere) but when you can, use them.

Find a Win-Win Solution

If you can calm yourself enough to think a situation through, you will often realize that there are ways to get out of it where both parties get what they want. This usually means reaching a compromise and learning how to communicate in a non-violent manner.

Take a Break

It's okay to step out of a situation that has become too intense instead of trying to muddle your way through it right then and there. Don't wait for the situation to escalate. Say something like, "Let's take a break. We can deal with this later."

Reassure Them

Misbehaving is often just a child's way of expressing his need for love and attention. It's not a sensible way of going about it, of course, but that is what many children can manage. If they knew how to express their needs in a more mature way, they would. But in the meantime, they don't. So make sure that your child knows that he is loved, that you are there for him when he needs you, and that you appreciate him for who he is.

Offer Choices

This is essential to raising children who will grow up to be independent, and able adults are letting them feel that they have a voice. Sometimes, even the choices that don't seem all that significant ("How do you want your eggs today?") help children feel that they have a say in what goes on around them. This is particularly beneficial for children who have recently undergone major life changes such as a move, parents divorcing, or the birth of a sibling.

Whisper

We are so used to a loud, noisy world where everyone and everything from the TV to our various gadgets are trying to get our attention by trying to out-shrill the next thing. In a sound-filled world such as ours, you'd be surprised to find out just how effective and refreshing a simple thing such as whispering can be. Whispering gets the child's attention (and what a nice break from the usual that would be for him) and calms the parent.

Go Outside

A change of scenery is often the very thing that both parent and child needs. Step out and have a picnic in the yard, play in the park, take a hike or a stroll, and visit friends. Even a short time out of the home can make a real difference.

Remember that Children Think in Pictures

Make specific instead of abstract requests: "Climb down slowly" instead of "Be careful!" "Stop jumping!" doesn't work because the action word "jumping" tends to drown out the word "stop." "Slow down!" will get through more easily.

Have a Sense of Humor

You wake up to Sophia pouring an entire box of cereal and an entire jug of milk into the dog's bowl. The image is so incredulous and frustrating and funny, and you're torn between laughing and yelling at her. Stop.

126

CHAPTER 17

BE TRUE TO YOURSELF

Taking Care of Yourself

Parenting, in itself, is a tough job. Parenting toddlers is super tough. While you struggle to handle that little bundle of energy, oftentimes, you forget about yourself. We are so invested in the well-being and care of our little one that our own health and mental sanity take a back seat.

Toddlers are energy driven, curious beings. With their curious nature and ever-developing emotional repertoire, they unwittingly throw many challenges before us. Understandably, such challenging behaviors can strain our patience to breaking point and frustrate us to no end. It becomes, therefore, even more, important that you take a breather every now and then so you do not lose your own balance and control of emotions. Remember that if you lose control of your emotions and get exceptionally angry over your child, not because they have done something so unpardonable, but because you are so frustrated with the continued stress of misbehavior that a point comes where your patience breaks, you will only harm your child more. As innocent as toddlers are, they are incapable of doing something unpardonable that would deserve or justify the use of force on your part. It is important, therefore, to act before the situation reaches that boiling point, that threshold where things could tip over for worse.

Controlled Reactions

The best step that you can take as a parent is to take care of your own emotions in a timely manner. If you are working hard and struggling to teach your child emotional control and addressing challenging behaviors, it all comes to nothing if you yourself end up losing control of your emotions.

Many times, we as parents are tempted to simply shout, slap, or yell at our children. But, if you wish to be a positive parent, take care that your actions or reactions to your child are hasty and rushed. Make it a point to breathe deeply (remember the breathing exercises!) and calm yourself before addressing your child. Count at least up to ten to give yourself time to calm your mind and swallow that frustration and anger. This is an important step to practice before you talk to your child after a difficult situation or as a reaction to their misbehavior. Imagine what you could do to your child if you did not calm yourself and take the time to think clearly and with positivity before approaching them. Keeping this thought, and this realization always at the forefront of your being as a parent will help you reign in your emotions and not act rashly.

Self-Care

Beyond providing consistent and controlled reactions each time to every misbehavior, it is important to make your own self-care a priority. Allot time for taking care of yourself each day. But what exactly is self-care? It is like filling up your tank before you begin each day fresh and rejuvenated. It is giving your mind and body the rest it deserves. It is to give yourself the ability to handle your own social and emotional needs as an individual and not just as a parent. Self-care might is the last thing on your mind now when all your focus is on your toddler and giving them your best. But, you can't really give them your best when you are not your hundred percent self. Think of the safety instructions on flights. They always say that if the pressure in the cabin drops, you must put on your oxygen mask first before assisting your child. Of course, our initial instinct is first to take

care of our child. But, if we do not get oxygen, we may pass out and will not be able to take care of our child or ourselves. The same goes for life. We must have our needs met so that we can care for our family properly. There are a few things that you can do to give yourself proper care. Plan to experiment with the different self-care strategies so you are able to decide what strategies work best for you.

Meditation

A short and quick meditation spell can help you feel refreshed. If you are new to the world of meditation, there are several resources available to guide you through various meditation techniques. Make a habit of meditating for at least five minutes every day, either in the morning or in the evening, so that you remain calm and rejuvenated every day. You can even include your child in your daily meditational episodes so that you both can benefit greatly from this important life skill.

Spending Time Outdoors

An excellent idea is to spend sufficient time outdoors near nature. It has been observed that simply watching the greenery for a certain period of time has a very soothing effect on the mind. Therefore, if you could squeeze time out to spend at least a little time per week at a place full of greenery, close to nature and its elements, it would be greatly calming and rejuvenating for you. Look for hillsides, riverbanks, mountain treks, waterfall resorts, or any such spots that you can easily reach for a quick refreshing trip. If once in a week is not workable for you, you could opt for other self-care techniques and keep outdoors to a minimum of once in a month or two.

Music

This is one of the easiest ways to stay calm and poised. Simply listen to any music that you like, which you are confident would calm you. You could listen to music at almost any time. Whether

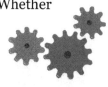

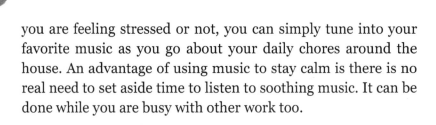

you are feeling stressed or not, you can simply tune into your favorite music as you go about your daily chores around the house. An advantage of using music to stay calm is there is no real need to set aside time to listen to soothing music. It can be done while you are busy with other work too.

Physical Exercise

Keeping physically active apart from all the work you do around the house will greatly help you stay fit and refreshed. A time and activity assigned explicitly for the purpose of the exercise will work positively on your mindset. If you are unable to hit the gym for some reason, simply taking a walk outdoors for at least fifteen minutes will do wonders for your positive approach to daily issues.

Maintain a Journal

If you are able to write your thoughts and feelings regularly in a diary or a journal, it would be greatly beneficial in relaxing you and emptying your mind of stressful thoughts and problematic issues. This can be a great tool to keep you positive and feeling good about your life. When things become tough, you can make it a point to just write down at least three things you are happy about and grateful for. This can become your own gratitude journaling exercise. It will help you retain a positive outlook on life and avoid feelings of excessive frustrations and annoyance.

Pamper Yourself

You could take time out to treat yourself with a few simple pleasures. These need not necessarily be luxuries. Simple things like an aromatic massage, a hot bath, some soothing music, lighting scented candles around the house, or drinking rejuvenating herbal teas can all be great ways to pamper yourself and give yourself some much-needed attention.

Spend Time with Family and Friends

If you can make time to get away from the busy schedules and the hustle and bustle of daily life to spend time with your friends, it would be a great way to unwind. Get some away time from kids by having someone watch over them while you take a much-needed breather. This will help you relax, and you will be able to get back in the groove after the retreat with more vigor and energy.

Get Away from Gadgets

Though it is usually assumed that watching something on your mobile or the television will help you relax, and it is valid to some extent, often times it is the contrary that is true. From one social app to another, you can simply feel stressed into replying to messages, emails, and whatnot. Instead, if you can spare time for a digital detox, it will be extremely beneficial for you.

132

CHAPTER 18

YOU MATTER

Children tend to suck up most of their parents' energies and time. However, You are not just a provider, a driver, a cooker, a carers. You matter. You have needs. Adult needs. And so is for your partner or any other adult helping raising your children. You need your space and time, and so does your partner. This is essential in order to be relaxed enough when reconnecting with your child.

You need to take care of your emotions with the aim of coaching your children's big emotions.

In case your parenting background has been particularly negative; for instance, you have survived narcissist parents or abuses, you need to re-parenting yourself and avoid bringing the past misdeeds into your relationship with your kids.

Attempting to raise children, especially those who tend to be disobedient or those who have been spoiled for many years, can be very difficult. It usually takes a lot of thought and self-control not to resort to the things we usually do, the parenting methods and statements that we grew up with, and the language that has been woven into us. For many parents, yelling, punishing, sarcasm, name-calling, and threats seem to be the only ways they can make themselves heard.

However, these aren't the only ways. Worse, they don't work. Child psychologists have repeatedly pointed out that punishment, yelling, and discipline tactics that aim to subjugate chil-

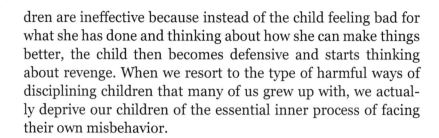

dren are ineffective because instead of the child feeling bad for what she has done and thinking about how she can make things better, the child then becomes defensive and starts thinking about revenge. When we resort to the type of harmful ways of disciplining children that many of us grew up with, we actually deprive our children of the essential inner process of facing their own misbehavior.

How to Stop Feeling Anxious and Guilty About Your Parenting Skills

It is impossible to be the best parent, you are capable of being when you do not take time to set your mindset. Regardless of how patient you typically are or how well you can manage stress, every parent has a breaking point. This breaking point is a stressful moment, where you are overwhelmed with your little one's behavior and at a loss for what to do makes it any better. Of course, that breaking point may come easier when you have added stress from work, finances, or home life, as well as when you are hungry or tired. You see, the key to being the best parent you can be sure you are in the right mindset first. This involves taking care of yourself and being sure you have the alone time you need to recharge when it's needed.

You Cannot Pour from an Empty Cup

It is not uncommon for new parents to feel they must dedicate every waking moment to their child. They are constantly interacting with their little ones during their waking hours and desperately trying to catch up on housework when they are asleep. While there is nothing wrong with being dedicated to your baby and home life, you cannot pour from an empty cup. Even parents who are at work during the day need time to 'refill their cup,' meaning they need to take care of themselves before they have the energy stores to care for others.

Finding time for yourself is about more than hygiene or relaxation. It is about finding time to nurture your relationship with

your significant other, getting away for relaxation with friends, and getting time away from their toddler. Whereas babies require constant supervision, toddlers can play in safe environments with less supervision. Allowing them to play on their own also encourages their individualism and independence. These are things that allow them to explore and develop their personality traits. Allowing them to play on their own also allows you to observe your little one and the way they interact with their environment.

Strengthening the Bond Between Mom and Dad

Though not all toddlers grow up in a two-parent home, those that do should see mom and dad as a unified front. A major part of staying on the same page is finding time to nurture your relationship. You should feel comfortable talking to your partner about the blessings and pitfalls of parenting. They should support you in finding time for yourself to recharge. They should also be willing to spend time with your toddler, helping them learn more about the world around them, and sharing in the parenting experience.

The key to finding any type of coherence between mom and dad is having a strong relationship that you can build cooperation on. Make time for each other—not just to talk about your child, but to talk to each other and become closer. Get in the habit of relying on your partner. Be clear about your own needs and how they can help. Getting time away from your little one is also crucial for effective parenting. Parents in loving relationships need time to celebrate and grow their love to maintain a strong, supportive bond. Make the time for your partner. Of course, your toddler is more demanding and has greater needs. After all, they rely on you to cook for them, help them clean up, provide them guidance, and much more. Be sure your partner is not being pushed away in the meantime. You'd be surprised how much having a date night twice a month and spending a little bit of time without your toddler each night (even if it's cuddling and

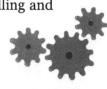

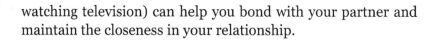

watching television) can help you bond with your partner and maintain the closeness in your relationship.

Get Enough Sleep

People often imagine new parents as those with dark circles under their eyes, unkempt hair, and stains on their t-shirt, walking like zombies in a sleep-deprived stupor. It can be difficult to be sure you are getting enough sleep, especially when your little one is not sleeping through the night yet. Fortunately, the toddler years come with an increased likelihood that your little one will not wake up for a middle-of-the-night feeding. You'll be able to get a few more hours of uninterrupted sleep than you did when they were an infant.

If you don't get enough sleep at night, find time to nap with your toddler during the day. Many new parents say this is easier said than done, as there is always something to do. Once the baby is down for a nap, it is easy to find yourself binging your favorite television show or trying to catch up on housework. Keep in mind that the television show and the messy house will still be there when you wake up. Try to at least rest your body while your little one is napping. Ideally, try to fit in some meditation or mind relations. Find some relating tracks that you love listening to and enjoy the feeling of mindfulness when your little one wakes up again. If you cannot afford a cleaner, try to do little and often. This might help you feel that you are at it, and the house is tidy (for your sanity). This also might prevent you from ending up having hours of house chores to carry out while having a toddler (or more) around. Another idea could be to stick a list of house chores to do in your kitchen and ask your partners, and/or other carers, to help tick them off the list while the day goes along. Another valuable option to consider is to see house chores as an activity to perform With your toddler(s). Toddlers love to be given jobs. We are obviously not suggesting child labor but! A simple house chores that they can be completely absorbed with while you are praising them for being

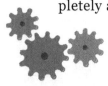

helpful, can buy you that 15 mins to clean a toilet, peel those vegetables or sort the laundry. Think strategically!

Do the Things That Make Life Simpler

Some parents feel bad about taking the 'easy road' for their toddlers. However, what they don't realize is that there are things that you can do that are easier without compromising your child's care. Additionally, doing things a simpler way gives you more time. This means you have more time for doing crafts and interacting with your little one. You also have more time to yourself—which is critical to maintaining your sanity. Here are a few strategies used by those parents whom we would classify as 'experts.' They'll free up your time without sacrificing how effectively you are raising your toddler.

Take Advantage of Low-Maintenance Cooking

Crock Pots can be a lifesaver for parents, especially when they have errands, cleaning, or work to worry about during the day. Instead of stressing about dinner, you can throw meat, veggies, sauces, and whatever else you would like into the crock pot and let it cook on low. You don't have to worry about constantly stirring it or overcooking the meat, as this method of cooking lets many flavors meld together. There are tons of recipes available online if you don't know where to get started!

Find Things to Do That Include Your Toddler

There is nothing wrong with working out with your toddler in the room or putting them in a stroller and taking them for a jog. Another great tool plays dates. The other child will help your little one to socialize and give them something to do while you catch up with the other child's parent. This allows you to have a good time while encouraging your child's social development.

Join a Gym with a Playroom

Once your child is old enough, it can be useful to join a fitness center that has a playroom or sign up for classes designed for mums to bring their children with them, such as running buggies, mummy fit, and so on. Of course, you should always ensure the safety of the environment and the credentials of the play area supervisor before leaving your little one in their care. There are two major benefits to these types of centers. First, you get some alone time with your little one close by—but out of the way. Second, your toddler has the chance to interact and socialize with other kids in their age group.

Familiarize Your Toddler with Friends and Relatives

Children look to their parents for everything. They share a special bond from the moment they are born and all through their life. Even so, your toddler must have the chance to interact with family members and friends. These people form your support system. They are the people that you can trust your toddler with when you want to spend alone time with your significant other—or even if you just need a break. Starting these bonds early is important to preventing toddler freak-outs when mom or dad leaves the house.

Keep Your Little One Busy

A busy toddler is a well-behaved toddler (for the most part). When kids are busy, they are learning. Additionally, activities keep your toddler from falling into the trap of electronics like televisions, iPads, and other devices. You'll learn more about great activities for your toddler and family, as well as how to set limits and rules about screen time.

Set Boundaries

Your toddler is constantly picking up on new words that describe the world around him or her. While it is exciting as your

little one learns new words, especially at first, it can be frustrating when they are rambling on, and you are trying to have a little quiet time. Keep in mind that your child is just now learning about all that goes on around them. They are going to have questions and want reassurance about the things they believe in the world. Their conversation is also an incredible learning experience, as they look to you for guidance on what is going on in their world.

Even though, you should help your little one as they explore, you should also get in the habit of setting boundaries for your toddler. This is especially true for stay-at-home parents and the child's primary caretaker. Let them know when you need a little time for yourself. Encourage them to play and explore on their own.

Eat a Well-Rounded Diet

On top of lacking sleep, many new parents do not eat the nutrition they need. It is so much easier to grab a handful of chips or a quick sandwich or microwavable meal, rather than preparing something healthy and nutritious. Besides, who has time to eat with all the demands that parenting has?

If you pay close attention that you binge on chips for lunch or make other unhealthy choices, you'll notice that the food you are eating is not nourishing your body. It may make you feel overfull, bloated, or sluggish. You may feel unfocused or tired. This is no way to be in the best possible state of body and mind for parenting.

Additionally, countless studies have proven that eating a healthy diet is essential for proper functioning and brain health. The foods that we eat provide the nutrition we need to thrive. Without it, parents might become agitated easier, which hinders their ability to think clearly and rationally when dealing with a cranky toddler.

140

CHAPTER 19

SEVEN STEPS TO PEACEFUL PARENTING

Step One: The Peace Within

Icannot emphasize enough the role of parents. Your role should be as a role model—pun intended. We expect our child to grow up as emotionally stable adults, but their highly impressionable minds are constantly taking silent queues from us, whether we intend for this or not. One of the most attractive and successful traits in any person is emotional intelligence. This means that we should be able to regulate our feelings in the face of distress, anger, fear, and even disappointment.

Think back to the example of implementing a subtle form of meditation in your day when you run short of time. This will be difficult in the beginning, but you can use the motivation from seeing your child thrive in adulthood as a passion for practicing silence and regulation. Commit yourself to the parental "stop, drop, and roll."

Let's say your child is throwing a major tantrum in the super-market, and your face is turning blood red. Turn your attention to your breathing and listen to the sound of air passing through your respiratory tract. Breathe deeply three times and look around you to identify five objects. What can you see? What can you hear? What can you smell? What can you feel? Finally, what can you taste in your mouth? The last one might not always be

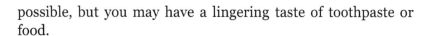

possible, but you may have a lingering taste of toothpaste or food.

Use your five senses to bring yourself back to the present before you erupt like Vesuvio. This happens fast and jerks you back to here and now so that your brain can process information and feelings quickly to handle the situation without yelling at the top of your lungs. It prevents us from reacting in a way we regret, and your child is not scorned with a reprimand.

I want to share a fun science fact with you before we move on. Self-control is an innate skill we all have, and certain practices can improve it dramatically (Self-Control, n.d.). Our ability to regulate our impulses reside in our prefrontal cortex, and this is how we solve problems, regulate emotions, and choose our responsive behavior. Activating and training this part of the brain can lead to a volume increase in your gray matter. Yes, we can grow the size of our brains. Emotional regulation is another skill we need to learn, and if we can change the size of our brains, why can't we change the content of it?

Step Two: Familial Connections

Connecting with your child is another topic I have brushed before, but I will expand a little further now. Let me tell you once more that peaceful parenting is not possible if you do not have a bond with your child. It will complicate matters if you simply drop punishment from the table because your child still will not have the motivation required to do the right thing. They will see you as a pushover who has gone soft and take advantage of you every chance they get.

The first thing you do is dedicate 15 minutes a day with each child. This time is for the two of you, and you can do anything. Small children love bedtime stories, and you can create a night-time ritual in which you act out the scenes from their favorite storybook. Spend time doing what they love and keep a close physical bond. Do not forget their goodnight kisses and tuck them in comfortably. Teenagers can be more

complicated, but you can get involved in their hobbies and support them.

You can explain what is happening once you have established a considerable bond. Sit them down and speak to them about the changes taking place. Ask them if they have noticed that you yell less now and welcome them on board to the new family plan. Make them feel appreciated and acknowledged by asking them straight out for their cooperation. This might take more than one tries.

Step Three: Limitations

Punishment is off the table, so how do you discipline your child? This will only work if you have created a bond of trust between you. You have had that conversation in which you discussed the new strategy in your home, and there is no need to change the rules. The previous step, combined with compassion, allows you to see your child's point of view now, and that is a good thing. A family is a unity of people who work together, and there is no need for one person to be miserable to make everyone else happy. However, limits are the only way you discipline your child now.

Bedtime is a limit, and you can practice empathy by telling your child, "I know you'd love to play more, but you won't have the energy to play tomorrow if you burn it all up tonight." You have seen and acknowledged their desire to continue playtime before you reminded them of the rule of bedtime. Limits play a huge role in discipline, and if you have followed the steps thus far, your child is more likely to collaborate with you.

Step Four: Reparation

This relates strongly to old habits again because a job will feel unfinished if you let something go that would normally be punished. Another new habit for the collection you have gathered so far is to learn to repair rather than punish. It will also give you closure on a situation and avoid leaving you feeling incomplete. I suppose in those terms, this one is for the parents' benefit.

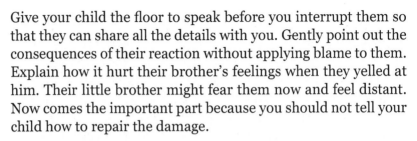

Give your child the floor to speak before you interrupt them so that they can share all the details with you. Gently point out the consequences of their reaction without applying blame to them. Explain how it hurt their brother's feelings when they yelled at him. Their little brother might fear them now and feel distant. Now comes the important part because you should not tell your child how to repair the damage.

Ask your child how they think it can be repaired. You are not forcing an apology. This responsibility you hand to your child will empower them when they are free to correct things themselves. Talk about a relationship struggle you might have had with a friend and how you repaired it. Try and inspire them to do the right thing without instructing them. They will relish their own make-up with their sibling when they decide how to do it.

There can be resistance from your child, and this is when you need to help heal from their pains further. Make sure that you are speaking from an example and seeing things from their viewpoint.

Step Five: Dealing with Emotions

Emotions are inevitable, but you can respond differently. Children are developing automatic responses, and every time a "bad" emotion gets them into hot water, they learn from this and begin suppressing their feelings instead. Accumulating emotions is the worst thing possible because your child will explode when they are provoked at the wrong time. Punishment is the reason kids repress their feelings because they become afraid of showing them.

It will take plenty of connection time to overcome this. Watch a sad movie with your child and never tell them they are not allowed to cry. Allow your tears to flow with theirs. I knew a man who used to tell his son that it was inappropriate to laugh alone. He would refer to "crazy" people who laugh for no reason.

Besides creating an emotionally friendly environment, you can encourage good behavior with appreciation. Tell your child how

proud you are that they handled the situation correctly. Explain how it pulled your heartstrings when you saw their reaction to the homeless man. Make your child want to repeat their behavior by giving them recognition and appreciation for it.

Step Six: The Safety Net

Parents are supposed to be the safety net for their child when they go through life's traumas. Adulthood does not make us immune to distress, and even we still need someone to be our shoulder to cry on. I want my child to feel as though they can tell me anything, even when they are 30 years old. There is one trick to this, though, and it goes back to your emotional regulation. You need to react to something your child tells you and remain calm. The moment you respond aggressively or out of disappointment, you break the bond, you have worked so hard to create.

Think of it as walking on thin ice. Our child experiences trauma differently than us, and they might not have the coping mechanisms that we do. They can break down and sink into a hole of depression or anxiety. Continue expressing compassion and wait until your child opens to you. You might be able to see the surface of the scar, but you cannot always see what caused it.

Our child often turns to anger to cope with their fears or insecurities that formed from past wounds. It does not matter how mad they get; you stay tranquil and wait for them to share with you. Anger cries have a healing effect on their own. Haven't you noticed how much better you feel after a good cry? Encourage the flow of tears so that they can release those hurtful emotions inside of them.

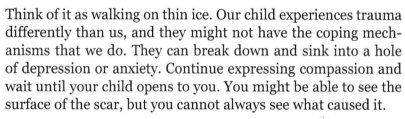

146

CONCLUSION

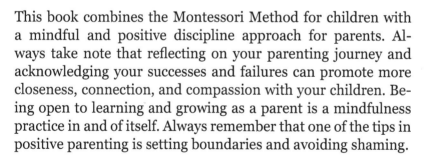

Thank you for making it to the end. By now, you should have gained a good understanding of the Montessori approach and how it can be implemented in the home. Unlike the traditional classroom and parenting style, where the adult tells the child what to learn, do, be, and when, the Montessori approach is a ground-breaking way that encourages independence from an early age. The adult doesn't dictate to the child about what they need to know, nor do they punish the child for not learning or for not being interested in what is taught. The traditional style of learning is quite conflicting. For instance, children are expected to start talking, walking, and moving about by the time they are toddlers. Yet, when they start to do those things, they are reprimanded for it. They are told to "be quiet" and "keep still."

This book combines the Montessori Method for children with a mindful and positive discipline approach for parents. Always take note that reflecting on your parenting journey and acknowledging your successes and failures can promote more closeness, connection, and compassion with your children. Being open to learning and growing as a parent is a mindfulness practice in and of itself. Always remember that one of the tips in positive parenting is setting boundaries and avoiding shaming.

Very few people question this way of bringing up children. However, over the century, there have been some people who have questioned it and then gone on to create something innovative. Dr. Maria Montessori is one of those people. She created the Montessori Method, which has become increasingly popular in recent years thanks to well-known public figures like Amazon founder Jeff Bezos and Google founder Larry Page, both

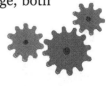

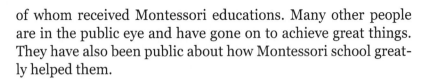

of whom received Montessori educations. Many other people are in the public eye and have gone on to achieve great things. They have also been public about how Montessori school greatly helped them.

The Montessori Method educates children to be self-directive by allowing them to participate in hands-on activities that are fun, stimulating, and collaborative. The activities a child undertakes are designed to engage their five senses of touch, taste, smell, sound, and sight. Dr. Montessori found that when these senses are stimulated through activities, it increases a child's intellectual development. She carried out a large amount of research on how children learn and behave. She found that up to the age of six, a child is very susceptible to their environment. This is an important time because whatever they learn at this point will impact how they show up in the world as adults. If they are nurtured, encouraged, supported, and raised in a safe environment, they are highly likely to grow up as confident, balanced adults. The Montessori Method will help a child to:

- Become independent from an early age.
- Receive an education that is focused on child-centered learning.
- Be creative and imaginative.
- Develop self-control and self-discipline.
- Develop a high level of emotional and intellectual intelligence.
- Become socially confident.

As your child gets older, you are sure to discover more benefits. However, you may even notice them in your new-born.

Adults often forget that children are intelligent beings, so they address them as if they know very little and need talking down. However, by choosing to read this guide, you have started your journey on a different and amazing path. Your role as a Montessori parent is to be a guide to your child as they decide what they would like to learn. Their preferences for activities will change as they get older, and you will need to alter the Montessori home to reflect this. Children have a natural tendency

to want to learn, and they also have a desire to contribute to their household or the community at large. They just need to be encouraged to do these things. If you introduce them to practical life skills from an early age, they will want to contribute towards activities that are considered "boring" or "chores" to the non-Montessori child.

In this guide, you have learned about the guiding principles of the Montessori Method, which include:

- The child is free to explore his/her environment.
- The child is a master of his/her learning.
- The child learns through his/her senses.
- The child needs a safe and nurturing environment.

At the start of this guide, you may have had a lot of questions about how you, as a parent, could start to incorporate the Montessori principles into your child's life. This guide intends to leave you feeling more confident as you embark on your journey as a Montessori parent.

You now have the knowledge and the resources at your fingertips to be an empowering Montessori parent.

One of the biggest takeaways from this book is that the child should be free to explore their environment, and you must ensure the environment is safe for them to do so. For instance, your room/s should be childproof. If it means getting down on your hands and knees so that you can perceive things from your child's height, then please do so.

Another major message of this book is that you don't need to feel overwhelmed or stressed out about creating a Montessori home. Many parents are worried that because they have limited space or a tight budget, they aren't going to be able to design an ideal Montessori home or that they won't be able to get it "right."

There is no such thing as the "right" Montessori home because what will work for one parent and their child won't work for someone else. Also, you can create a stunning Montessori home without

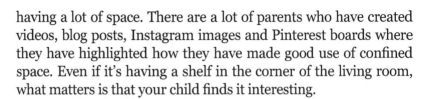

having a lot of space. There are a lot of parents who have created videos, blog posts, Instagram images and Pinterest boards where they have highlighted how they have made good use of confined space. Even if it's having a shelf in the corner of the living room, what matters is that your child finds it interesting.

It would be great for you to reach out and connect with other parents who believe in the Montessori movement. This will deepen your understanding of Montessori because you will be able to share insights, ask questions, and meet up for playdates.

The first six years of a child's life have them dipping in and out of sensitive periods. Sensitive periods are when children are even more impressionable with their environment. They take everything in like a sponge, so patience and consistency are needed at these times. But those investments will be worth it. You now have ideas for various activities that your child can do to develop through each sensitive period, which includes small objects, movement, order, senses, expressive language, and music. Each of these is very important and has significant benefits for the child.

If you are creative or on a budget, you can always make furniture, toys, etc. to suit your child's needs. Many of the blogs on Montessori parenting give tips and advice on how to make your resources and materials. I hoped to leave you with practical steps you can take to set up your Montessori home, and now you can go and start implementing what you have learned. Please do not feel like you have to integrate everything. It would not be practical or beneficial for you or your child. He should ideally have an environment that is clutter-free, organized, stimulating, and calm. They strongly desire order at this stage in their development because they are looking to understand the world and discover their identities. If your home is chaotic, it will be stressful for them. If you offer them too many activities at any given time, they will feel overwhelmed and will not be able to focus properly.

Your child will thrive with a few high-quality toys and activities that can always be rotated. The Montessori equipment and ma-

terials were designed for a reason—they support the Montessori approach. The floor bed, weaning table and chair, child-size utensils and furniture, etc., all allow the child to become independent and be more in control of their daily lives with you as their guide. However, you can substitute, so please don't worry about the cost of all this or where you will fit them in your home.

This is a lot of information to digest. Most of all, please take a moment to congratulate yourself for the effort you are putting into being the best parent to your child. Your choice today to bring Montessori into the home is going to serve your child well as he/she continues to journey through life, and while he/she develops into an independent, strong thinker. Your child will ultimately have you to thank for setting him/her off on that journey. Best of luck to you!

We're here because of you

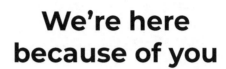

If you have found any value in this material, please consider leaving a review and joining the Author's Mission to give the most resourceful start to all children around the world

By scanning the QR-Code below ♥

★ ★ ★ ★ ★

SCAN ME

BIBLIOGRAPHY

Baumrind, D. (1966). Effects of Authoritative Parental Control on Child Behavior. Child Development, 37(4), 887-907. doi:10.2307/1126611

Hart, R., (2017). Toddler Discipline. La Vergne: Editorial Imagen LLC.

Hargis, A., and Sylvester B., (2018) Toddler Discipline for every age and stage. Effective strategies to tema tantrums, overcome challenges and help your child grow. Rockridge Press.

Montessori, M. (2004). The Montessori method: the origins of an educational innovation: including an abridged and annotated edition of Maria Montessori's The Montessori method. Rowman & Littlefield.

Montessori, M., (2010) The Montessori Method, Schocken.

Montessori, M., Hunt, J. M., & Valsiner, J. (2017). The Montessori method. Routledge.

Rucklidge J, Taylor M, Whitehead K. (2011) Effect of micronutrients on behavior and mood in adults with ADHD: evidence from an 8-week open label trial with natural extension. J Atten Disord. 15(1):79-91. doi: 10.1177/1087054709356173. Epub 2010 Jan 13. PMID: 20071638.

Sanders, M. R. (2008). Triple P-Positive Parenting Program as a public health approach to strengthening parenting. Journal of family psychology, 22(4), 506.

Seay, A., Freysteinson, W. M., & McFarlane, J. (2014, July). Positive parenting. In Nursing Forum (Vol. 49, No. 3, pp. 200-208).

Printed in Great Britain
by Amazon

26582165R00086